The poignantly written book is beneficial for people dealing with their partner's addiction and betrayal for several reasons: (1) the author's firsthand experience allows her to empathize with and understand the pain, confusion, and emotional turmoil that spouses in similar situations may be going through. (2) Lackey helps spouses understand the complexities and challenges associated with sexual addiction, including the impact it can have on relationships and families. By providing this insight, she helps spouses gain a deeper understanding of their partner's behavior and addiction, which can be crucial in the healing process. (3) Lackey shares her journey of healing and transformation, demonstrating that it is possible to move beyond victimization and survival toward a life of abundance and purpose. She provides practical advice, tools, and strategies to help spouses cope with their emotions, rebuild trust, and find their identity and purpose. (4) Lackey's book incorporates her faith and trust in God's faithfulness. This aspect of the book can provide additional support and guidance for individuals who find solace and strength in their spirituality. (5) Lackey creates an emotional connection with readers by including emotion-filled letters written to her spouse but never mailed. These letters allow spouses to relate to the raw emotions, pain, and anger that can arise in such situations. By sharing her vulnerability, Lackey helps spouses feel understood and validated in their own emotional journey.

—**Dr. Katherine Hutchinson-Hayes**, editor, speaker, podcaster, and author of *A Fifth of the Story, Focus: 45 Devotionals to Keep Jesus in the Picture*, and *God's Little Black Dress for Women*

Kathryn M. Lackey

LETTERS
from LOVE'S
BATTLEFIELD

Triumph *in the* Aftermath
of a Spouse's Sexual Addiction

- A MEMOIR -

BROOKSTONE
PUBLISHING GROUP

Birmingham, Alabama

Letters from Love's Battlefield

Brookstone Publishing Group
An imprint of Iron Stream Media
100 Missionary Ridge
Birmingham, AL 35242
IronStreamMedia.com

Library of Congress Control Number: 2024902223

Cover design by twolineSTUDIO.com

ISBN: 978-1-960814-07-4 (paperback)
ISBN: 978-1-960814-08-1 (eBook)

1 2 3 4 5—28 27 26 25 24

As I tell my story, I aspire
to awaken those inflicted by shame
through education and forgiveness,
to release them from the scars of sexual addiction,
and to reveal the beauty of the layered transformation
that lies within.

Contents

Dedication

This book is dedicated to my wonderful family members and friends who supported me throughout the writing of this book. With their understanding and encouragement as my foundation, I am inspired to tell my story to help others negatively impacted and wounded by the abuses of sexual addiction.

To my Dallas and Nashville families, thank you so much for loving and believing in me and God's timing for this book despite the demands of building a new business. His timing is never our own, but it is perfect toward His will.

To Katherine Hayes, this story could not have been born without your mentoring and coaching. I am so grateful to Iron Stream Media for pairing us to write this book. Your instruction and patience have helped to produce a message truly unique to the topic of abuse recovery.

To my good friends, Laureen and Janie, your support and encouragement have meant the world to me. Thank you for cheerleading me with each chapter.

To my deceased Aunt Jean, who once vowed to lock me in a closet until I produced a book, thank you for continuing to whisper my calling while God unveiled my happy ending.

And lastly, I dedicate this book to Kyle, our love story, and the memory of what once was. Thirty-eight years ago, I gave you my heart at the altar. I trusted the love of my life with all I had, including my dreams and hopes for our future.

To Kyle,

My beloved college sweetheart, the father of our three children, and the wonderful man I knew you to once be. I dedicate this book to you so that you may know beyond a shadow of a doubt that I loved you and could not imagine my life without you. We vowed to each other for better and for worse, and we achieved them both. With that, I lovingly say goodbye and let go of our past, the shackles and chains of victimization. May strength and forgiveness continue to be my guide.

With all my love,

Kathy

Preface

Fifteen years have passed since I sat in a courtroom of strangers and watched my ex-husband sentenced to twenty years behind bars for possession and solicitation of child pornography, felonies that failed to capture the full extent of his crimes. Our children have since grown and moved on. As I stood at the threshold of my life's next chapter, I instead found myself unexpectedly returning to my past as I prepared for his pending prison release at the onset of an isolating pandemic.

I froze as I read the notification letter of Kyle's forthcoming release. My survival instincts resurfaced, fearing the unknowns with many years of incarceration to premeditate his possible vengeance. With little time to prepare, I slept each night armed with a butcher knife beneath my mattress and a large candlestick at my bedside. Despite his long absence, I again fell victim to trauma and the uncertainty of his next move as he planned his return to society.

During this time, I also served as a co-facilitator of an adult DivorceCare group at my church, a Christian-based divorce support ministry for adults and children. During the two years that I served, I was blessed by the many testimonies of class participants committed to their grief walks through divorce, but the women's stories always moved me the most. Due to the impact of my personal divorce, I felt compassion for those women ruthlessly cast aside after decade-long marriages, especially those who sacrificed personal careers and financial independence for the betterment of their families. In the end, they were rewarded by their husbands' betrayals of unfaithfulness and sexual promiscuity. Although each story was individual, their pains and experiences paralleled those of my past.

While I was serving in this group and mentally processing my ex-husband's pending prison release, the clock ticked closer to the end of his sentence. With his return to society, I vowed to never again live in the shadows of his shame as a victim of my past. It was then that I reclaimed my future and relocated for a new beginning closer to family in Tennessee.

Finally, I'm healed!

"Not so fast," God said.

Though I'd moved to another state and started a new life and business, I discovered I wasn't on the other side of past hurts. A few months following my move, I answered the phone and received tragic news.

As I ended the call, I sat frozen. *Oh my gosh! He's dead.*

Something shocking had occurred. Just eight months after his prison release, Kyle fell to his death alone in a hotel room, defeated by the addiction that previously stole our family's present and future together.

Retrieving his will from my safe, I rediscovered forgotten letters of heartbreak I had written to him over a decade earlier but never mailed. Memories of my past became tears of regret. Through my faith, I knew God had a purpose for my journey, yet it remained unfulfilled all these years. I never understood why.

In the year that followed, I accepted Kyle's death as an unfortunate consequence of a serious, untreated addiction. I buried the past, as I had done for so many years. On a conscious level, I believed this acceptance to be successful. But God continued to nudge my heart. With each news media exposure of a high-profile sex offender facing judgment, God spoke to me. I hurt for the adults and children victimized by the abuses of the men they innocently trusted. I recalled my past journey to healing from the mental abuses and lies of a convicted sex offender, a man I once called my husband. It was during this time that God slowly helped me realize that the restless yearning in my soul was His timing and plan to share my testimony of a life blindsided by sexual addiction, then healed by His grace.

As I began to build a new life and business in a new state, I preferred to move on with my future. Yet, the yearnings grew stronger, and my writing began involuntarily. I finally accepted His calling and realized that silencing my story deprived hope to others who remained emotionally ostracized and tattooed by the shame of the sexual sinner. And that's where my story begins.

In the following pages, I share my testimony of a life-shattering trial conquered through the courage and strength that comes only through a personal faith in God and in oneself. Despite the devastations of a partner's sexual addiction, my path to healing and forgiveness reveals the restorative power of our loving Father.

My purpose for this book and my prayer is that God will use my story of recovery to help heal other lives affected by sexual addiction. I invite readers to see His provisions throughout the uncertainties and darkness of my path as He now fulfills my longtime prayer to turn something so bad into His ultimate good purpose.

Introduction

The years following my husband's conviction and incarceration for possession and solicitation of child pornography were a difficult journey. In the aftermath of his conviction, I pivoted my focus, delegating the legal implications of his felony to the court system while piecing together our family's brokenness. In the wake of this tragedy, we had become victims of his choices. What once seemed like picture-perfect lives had succumbed to the reality of Kyle's double life of depravity involving prostitution and child pornography.

My children and I became callous to publicity and embarrassment as we cautiously disengaged from others to dodge their judgments. The camouflage of our new normal disguised our grief and regret but challenged our efforts to succeed in school, work, and relationships as we tried to overcome and shield ourselves from his shame.

Behind a hidden addiction masked the image of a successful man enjoying an ideal career and family in a beautiful Dallas suburb. Our twenty-year marriage became a series of questions as I longed to understand the atrocities that now defined our reputation. *When did this addiction begin? How long has he been hiding his secret attraction to young girls? When did his craving for hookers magnify to a business of profit supported by greed?*

Those questions remained unanswered upon Kyle's death in November 2020. Upon his new taste of freedom, his addiction joined alcohol as it resurfaced following his release from prison.

Eight months later, he was found alone and dead in an empty hotel room. Gripped by its force, he sacrificed his life to sex and alcohol addiction, choosing a path of unrepentance for the lives he permanently changed as consequences of his choices.

In this country, sexual addiction is a growing phenomenon deteriorating our culture and values while fueling the destruction of marriages and families with temptations of cost-free viewing opportunities accessible through the internet. The National Library of Medicine has titled pornography use a national "porn-demic." Pornhub, the fourth most visited website in the US behind Google, YouTube, and Facebook, totaled over 2.14 billion global visits during a single month in 2023, more than Instagram, Netflix, Pinterest, and TikTok combined. In 2021, the US was categorized as the top consumer of pornography in the world, reporting over 68 million searches per month.

In all its illicit forms, our country's lust for sex and pornography replaces God's purpose for this union with unhealthy and perverted desires far removed from His intentions for expressions of love. As occasional temptations turn compulsive, innocent victims and families are left behind, overwhelmed by sadness, and struggle with family dysfunction, divorce, and addiction. They are left to question what's real and what's not as the addict's values decay into a spiral of narcissistic behavior to protect his secret obsession.

After my relocation to Tennessee, I repeatedly visited my past with each news media disclosure of high-profile celebrities indicted for sexual offenses. The list includes Bill Cosby, once my favorite comedian. I loved laughing with my family as a child as we watched episodes of *The Cosby Show*. Now, I can only see the facade of the comic celebrity who used his brand to conceal and manifest his narcissism in the acting community. In 2018, Cosby was convicted of aggravated indecent assault for the drugging and molesting of actress Andrea Constand in 2004. His crime sent him to prison until 2021.

In 2016, Larry Nassar, the former US Women's Gymnastics Team physician, was indicted for the depravation of over ninety talented, accomplished gymnasts at their Michigan training gym, including Olympic gymnasts Rachael Denhollander and Isabell Hutchins. In 2018, Nassar's accusers rose to 156. He received a sixty-year federal prison sentence for possession of child pornography. A second sentence would then follow for first degree criminal sexual misconduct. In turn, John Geddert, their coach, was also charged with multiple crimes, including sexual abuse and human trafficking. Geddert committed suicide on the day he was to turn himself over to the authorities.

The University of Michigan's Athletic Department team physician, Dr. Robert E. Anderson, was accused by several of his players of sexual misconduct during his 1967–1998 tenure. However, these accusations repeatedly went unpunished by former legendary head coach Bo Schembechler. In a media interview, Jon Vaughn, former University of Michigan football player and survivor of Dr. Anderson's sexual abuse, estimated that he experienced over forty sexual assaults by Dr. Anderson from 1988–1990. The university was forced to pay $490 million in legal settlements following Dr. Anderson's death in 2008.

And let's not forget Harvey Weinstein, a high-profile Hollywood producer, who was sentenced to twenty-three years for rape and sexual battery against multiple women.

The celebrity list continues with Jeffrey Epstein, financier, and his British partner, Ghislaine Maxwell, each accused of human trafficking and abuse of underage girls. Their social affiliations included Prince Andrew and presidents Bill Clinton and Donald Trump, who were reported visiting Epstein's publicized "sex mansion" on his island in the Caribbean. Authorities declared he took his own life in prison awaiting trial. His case lives on in the extradition of his business partner, Ghislaine Maxwell, now serving twenty years in prison for conspiring with Jeffrey Epstein to sexually abuse minors imported for the hospitality of visitors.

This list of the convicted unveils a phenomenon of the misuses of power and control to conceal sexual abuses while growing a trade industry rooted in sexual addiction. Its manifestation destroys lives and devastates victims. The ripple of destruction affects people in all social and economic demographics globally, and abuses to innocent victims are unlimited to the rich and famous.

Sexual addiction continues to grow at epidemic proportions, fueled by a new lifestyle of seclusion fostered by the Covid-19 pandemic. Our society also exploits and liberates sexual promiscuity, which includes recreational online viewings of porn. This continues to flourish a lucrative industry with US pornographic websites rivaling 2023 NCAA projected revenues of $1.15 billion. The United States is reportedly the leading global consumer of pornography, and yet, we remain ignorant of the negative dynamics and risks to children and families as sexual addiction lurks in the shadows of our everyday lives.

We are not strangers to the media profiles of this problem in the Catholic Church, veiled from public knowledge at the cost of the victims. And let us cry for the innocent child victims portrayed in Angel Studios' movie release *Sound of Freedom*, trafficked from other lands by pimp brokers to then be sold as commodities for sexual exploitation at ages too young to accept as reality.

As my husband defended his actions before his attorney as an accused sex offender, I felt like I'd met the devil himself, masked as my husband. I still recall his cold eyes piercing through mine as I listened in disbelief to his confession in his lawyer's office. It was as if his personality had morphed over time, and the man his family and friends once knew changed into someone unrecognizable.

While rebuilding my life after his conviction, I conquered

fear, insecurity, and shame. However, it was a constant struggle to create renewed confidence and security while providing stability for my family. Despite the challenges, a loving God held my hand throughout that journey, providing for me and my children through a personal walk of self-discovery.

Today, I have pushed the reset button, defining a future vision for a new life and business. I am also proud and blessed that each of my children have successfully resolved their hurts and accomplished college degrees and rewarding careers. God is so faithful, and I thank him for guiding me through my valley of darkness so I can share my testimony with the intention to help others along their healing journeys.

Chapter 1

The Day of Infamy

Verse of Reflection

You intended to harm me, but God intended it for good to accomplish what is now being done, the saving of many lives.

—Genesis 50:20

*T*here are some days in history when you remember the exact hour and location you received *the* news. Whether it was an unexpected death, an accident, or the calamity of the Twin Towers' destruction by terrorists, you remember the exact moment when the news unfolded and what you were doing. For me, that day occurred on December 5, 2005, at 8:30 a.m.

I remember standing at the kitchen island, cleaning up after preparing breakfast for the kids that Monday morning. Earlier, Kyle left for work as I drove our kids to school. We were resuming our normal weekday routine after returning from vacation, and I was cleaning up the kitchen as I readied to begin my day. Then, the phone rang. I saw Kyle's name on the caller ID. As I picked up the phone, he began the conversation with, "I lost my job."

"What? What happened?" I asked.

"I've been accused of a security breach. They just walked me out of the building." He remained calm and collected, but I detected reservation in his voice.

"What does that mean? What kind of security breach?" I replied. I was confused. Employed as a database manager at a telecom company for many years, my husband was privy to confidential company information, and there were strict protocols in place to protect client information from threat.

"My computer was confiscated while we were in Lake Tahoe, and they believe I've breached security," Kyle replied stoically. "I'm on my way home now. We'll talk about it more when I get there."

After he hung up, I waited anxiously for him to return home.

Our family had just returned from our twentieth wedding anniversary trip to Lake Tahoe accompanied by our son, then age eleven, and daughter, age fourteen. Although I'd kept my feelings from my family, secretly, our vacation was terrible for me. My intention was to mask my heartache from the kids during our family times together. As I realized my emotional struggle to remain married, Kyle's presence became increasingly painful and an effort to enjoy our celebration amid our relationship's continual decline.

Our Lake Tahoe trip had been originally planned both as an anniversary celebration and as a fun way to adapt to our new lives in Texas, where we had relocated for Kyle's job following the closure of his company's Raleigh, North Carolina, office. While we struggled with this unwanted transition, we both had hoped that within three years, the economy would improve, allowing our return to Raleigh, where we truly wanted to live and raise our children. But rather than begrudge our new home in Dallas, I focused on the positive opportunities provided to me as a full-time mom and caregiver, free to focus on my family and an aging mother. Much like during our military days when we were first wed, my intention was to use this relocation as an opportunity to explore Western places while "stationed" in our new land. I viewed Dallas not as much our new home as our current location. As a former military wife, I accepted Kyle's assignment and made it work best to fit our family knowing I could make the most out of our temporary residence.

Two years earlier, in 2000, we'd settled into our "forever" home north of Raleigh in a beautiful golf community in Wake Forest, North Carolina. This home presented a fresh beginning for us after our eldest son, Ryan, passed away suddenly in 1996 at age five. This was a change we sorely needed. Within the two years that followed, our family experienced the death of two parents and a brother, all unexpectedly, accompanied by a wrongful death lawsuit surrounding Kyle's brother's tragedy. I called the building of this new home my grief project. However, it seemed much more mine than Kyle's, due to his travels for business and executor responsibilities. I was the rock that kept our family running in his absence, and our individual roles synced harmoniously.

Our two remaining children were also healing from our family's losses through the additional loving support of friends and the community. We had also adopted a dog we lovingly called Angel Maxx, a male golden retriever who brought healing into our home through his unconditional happiness and "canine therapy."

Despite a fresh start in our new home, our marriage began to decline, and I became discouraged and hurt as Kyle emotionally drifted further and further away. The increasing disconnects with my husband left me slowly drowning in an emptiness that went continually unresolved. In my sorrow and confusion, I had come to a crossroads where I began privately contemplating divorce despite my financial fears as a stay-at-home mom.

It was through the loss of my child, Ryan, that I found God. As my faith walk through grief strengthened in the years that followed, I prayed for guidance and was continually led back into the battle for my marriage. Then, the economic downturn after 9/11 resulted in multiple job losses across the dot-com and IT sectors of the Research Triangle Park. When Kyle announced his options to accept either a severance package or a relocation with the closure of his company's Raleigh office, I was resentful. Following much prayer, I relinquished my new home to God's plan and recommitted to my marriage, trusting that this fresh start signified healing and a new beginning for our family amid our losses.

However, my husband's changes became much more apparent following our relocation. I became depressed and eager to discover the source of his disengagement and behaviors I deemed atypical for the man I had known and loved since college. Yet, I consistently failed to find answers. While I was patient with his withdrawal realizing his need to heal from our many losses and an unwanted transition, our intimate life was nonexistent. His lack of engagement and attention in our relationship eroded my confidence in our marriage. Hurting, I began to question the long-term commitment of my husband whom I no longer knew. Kyle was a proud and loyal man. He continued to provide for us and to act as if everything remained normal, but I knew he was struggling with emotions far deeper.

After our first year in Dallas, we finally resorted to marriage counseling. Kyle claimed he was wholeheartedly committed to our relationship's recovery, but instead, used logic and sarcasm to cast doubt toward my own mental stability. He dismissed his peculiar behaviors rationalizing each of my questions with a curt and mocking response.

"Kathy, think about it," he said in a demeaning tone. "I go to work, the gym, and then home. You know where I am 24/7. You know where every penny of our money goes. So where would I have the time or money to cheat on you?"

While those things were all true, they did not explain the unrest I felt in response to his new atypical behaviors. My instincts left me continually restless about the changes I saw in him. He claimed my suspicions were unwarranted, causing my self-confidence to erode as I began to second-guess myself. *Was I falling into chronic depression? Why did I feel so insecure?*

Each night, I watched Kyle's demeanor become steadily more perplexing. After more than twenty years with this man, I knew his normal routine and behaviors. Yet, he slowly fell into new patterns. He began falling asleep in his chair most evenings during our usual family time with the kids. As if drugged, he'd remain unconscious as his drink spilt into his lap, dripping down his leg into a puddle at his feet. He would then awaken hours later, disoriented, bumping into walls, and babbling as he stumbled to bed. He wasn't intoxicated, but was he on drugs? I became annoyed and wondered, *Why is he acting this way and continually so exhausted?*

Kyle had an answer to all my questions, and he dismissed his uncharacteristic behaviors with viable explanations. During the nights, I often rolled over in bed to discover him gone. He would return to bed several hours later feeling exhilarated after his new routine midnight snack.

During the day, I questioned his need for private phone conversations in strange places such as the bathroom and the garage. While I still trusted him, I could not explain his many perplexing behaviors, which left me more mystified than suspicious of potential adultery. His entire demeanor and character transformed after moving to Dallas, and I would soon learn that he was carrying the burden of a secret life.

Our arguments over his strange behavior resulted in distractions of romantic gifts, including wine and flowers, which worked for a time. He routinely arrived home around 6:30 p.m., dropped his gym clothes in the laundry room washer, and greeted me with a kiss on the nape of my neck as I prepared our family's dinner. While we worked on our marriage, I forced myself to trust the man I believed held our future. Despite my conflicts and questions, I continued to yearn for that greeting each night as security that we were okay, and that our marital problems were a mere phase that would soon find resolution.

When I think back to that fateful phone call when Kyle delivered the unexpected news of his job loss, I was completely unprepared. However, I was not worried. In the past, Kyle and I had always survived the unexpected, emerging with an even stronger emotional bond. I believed and trusted him totally and completely. I confidently believed we would rise above this trial successfully, just as we had through many others during our twenty years together, and that this misfortune would be no different.

"Kyle, everything will be okay. I'm sure of it," I said, fully believing the words I spoke. "This could be an opportunity for us to return to Raleigh. We never meant to stay in Texas. None of us have adjusted to our new lives here. We are fine financially, and you have so many choices. This could be an opportunity for you to begin consulting and start something new. We will be fine. I'll see you when you get home."

Thirty minutes later, Kyle walked through the garage door into the kitchen, where I met him. I stood there, silent, ready to support him in his discouragement. He looked at me as he entered the room.

"You want to tell me exactly what happened?" I finally asked.

Ignorant of the truth, that moment began a sequence of lies that peeled away like an onion skin, day by day, one layer at a time as my husband's hidden compulsions were slowly exposed.

Years earlier, following our son's death, Kyle poured his efforts into his career. I never challenged his grief journey because he supported mine, and I understood that people handle emotions in different ways. While Kyle appeared to have channeled his grief into his career, he had also chosen to numb his pain with an illicit lifestyle that would now come to surface.

Until then, Kyle blamed his job loss on his company's accusations of a security breach. Still ignorant of his double life, I continued to support him.

"Listen, Kyle. You have so many connections in this industry," I reminded him. "It won't take you long to find another job, or you can consider consulting. You're in a high-demand industry. In the past, you transitioned easily by making a few phone calls. This will be no different if a new job is what you want. Why don't you start calling a few people you know?"

While I was concerned about our new situation, I knew Kyle would land in a better career from this misfortune. He was a man of intelligence, loved by many for his jovial and magnetic personality who had many friends both inside and outside of work. His natural charisma attracted others instantly and remained qualities about him that I, too, had always loved and admired.

He nodded in agreement with my advice. But something different happened that day. Kyle picked up the phone and started calling his closest work allies, but no one would accept his calls then or the days that followed. Instead, they were distant and unresponsive. I found this very odd. Still, given the situation, they may have been uncomfortable talking to him directly until the corporate security breach accusations were resolved.

I realized I was wrong as the truth began to unravel.

In the weeks that followed, the Christmas season came and went. I don't remember much about the holidays, other than my mother's visit as the shock of truths began to unfold. I only recall the deep, dark revelations of a person I thought I knew.

"What's really going on, Kyle?" I asked him sternly. "After several weeks now, why is no one willing to take your call?"

By my tone, he realized it was time for his game of charades to come to an end.

He led me into our bedroom to speak privately, away from Mom. He sat down in our bedroom chair. "I've been accused of downloading pornography at work," he finally admitted.

With that, he began to disclose the truth. Enormous amounts of pornography had been discovered on Kyle's work computer, intentionally downloaded through the fax lines to bypass the company's firewalls. As security personnel passed his cubicle, the sound of moans made them suspicious of illicit activity, and they immediately reported this to Kyle's direct supervisor. During our trip to Lake Tahoe, security was ordered to investigate his hard drive contents and downloads. It was then that they discovered more than two thousand images of minors. Kyle's offenses suddenly escalated to a felony level. The FBI then confiscated the computer as criminal evidence at which point criminal charges for possession of child pornography became imminent.

I became nauseated by his admissions. I felt like I was trapped in a nightmare. My waking hours were filled with fear of the unknown and an uncertain future. An indictment would follow, and soon, my husband's secret life would be exposed to our new neighbors and friends. As the rock of our family, I fell into my codependent role to control my husband's downward spiral and protect our family legally. Not knowing exactly where to turn, I called the divorce attorney I'd hired six months earlier. At that time, I fully intended to leave my husband, exhausted from the deterioration of our marriage. He referred me to the best criminal attorney in the city. I called the referral, explained Kyle's charges, and made an appointment. The $10,000 retainer was my earnest money for our family's survival.

Kyle and I arrived at Mr. Cavanaugh's office the following morning. We sat adjacent to one another as Mr. Cavanaugh sat down behind his desk and asked Kyle for his complete story, withholding nothing. The lawyer remained silent, void of emotion as he listened to my husband's confessions.

I sat transfixed as Kyle confessed to unfathomable crimes that went far deeper than collections of child pornography. I learned of his private online email group, a secret list he had cultivated but relinquished to avoid further scrutiny by the authorities. He then admitted to operating his second business from the office of our home as his family slept.

The attorney probed further to unveil the group's purpose and to reveal the members' identities. Kyle conceded that his subscriber list comprised doctors, lawyers, and politicians with high public profiles, too affluent for Kyle to risk disclosures. He provided them online reviews on the dark web to promote new prostitutes for an escort agency in exchange for his own patronage discounts. When they traveled through Dallas, he met with them at lunch to recommend suitable prostitutes to fulfill their deepest desires.

The attorney and I sat frozen as Kyle introduced us both to his secret life as a white-collar pimp. His lies unraveled like the skins of an onion. Eventually, the onion's core produced enough vapor to overcome my eyes with tears, unable to breathe as I was thrust into his double life of depravity. The shroud began to fall and disclose his many dark secrets. I felt nothing but shock and bewilderment. *How could this have happened in my world on my watch?*

When Kyle finished his shocking confession, I opened my mouth to speak.

Kyle turned and angrily glared at me. "You shut up! You're only here because I allowed you to be."

At that moment, I felt as if I'd met Satan himself as I stared into my husband's cold, dead pupils. The caring, jovial, soft green eyes that had always drawn me in were then filled with darkness and evil surfacing like oil against water.

Mr. Cavanaugh excused himself to make a phone call to the district attorney. With tears streaming down my cheeks, I knelt at Kyle's side, trembling at the discovery of this other person living inside him. As his old self transfigured into malevolence, my heart was crushed in my love for him and who he had now become.

"What happened to you? How is this real?" I asked, feeling helpless how to now help the man I loved all these years.

Kyle remained despondent. I could sense his trepidation of the consequences to his crimes, but he remained calm, justified, and unrepentant.

Finally, Mr. Cavanaugh returned, and I returned to my seat.

"As Kyle's presiding attorney," the lawyer said. "I made a call to the district attorney and was able to persuade him to reduce a possible twenty-year conviction based on your clean background and no past criminal records. You've been offered a $10,000 fine and will be required to carry an ID card identifying you as a registered sex offender throughout a ten-year probation. You will no longer be allowed within a proximity of five hundred feet of any child, and supervision will be always required around your own children. Do you agree to these terms? Your other option is to face a potential twenty-year conviction for possession and solicitation of child pornography."

Mr. Cavanaugh left the room again to give us time to talk. I encouraged Kyle to accept the offer. Theoretically, the district attorney graced my husband with a "get out of jail free" card.

But Kyle had other plans.

"I never touched a child," he responded with scorn in his hardened tone. "Others have done far worse than me."

As I witnessed his response to the gravity of his crimes, I was forced to realize an even more severe problem that required a prompt decision, one which would change the trajectory of our family forever.

Chapter 2

Depression's Warning

Verse of Reflection

*It is God who arms me with strength
     and keeps my way secure.
He makes my feet like the feet of a deer;
     he causes me to stand on the heights.
He trains my hands for battle;
     my arms can bend a bow of bronze.
You make your saving help my shield,
     and your right hand sustains me.
     your help has made me great.
You provide a broad path for my feet
     so that my ankles do not give way.*

—Psalm 18:32–36

$\mathcal{A}$s I digested the new discoveries of Kyle's unspeakable and unfathomable confessions, which would transform our lives, I reminisced about our past in Raleigh, North Carolina, and our history leading to that day.

After our son's death, the most difficult part of the grieving process was watching our marriage slowly die. It was silent but progressive, almost undetectable. The first few years, we were supportive of each other's pain when we were together. Each of us had a personal outlet that got us through a moment, a day, or a birthday. Every day was unique, and our responses to that uniqueness defined our individual pain and coping mechanisms.

I could never truly define Kyle's coping outlet. I suspected he avoided healing from his pain as he instead focused on distractions including his fatherhood tasks, "honey-do" chores, or work. Despite his travels and obligations, on the surface, he appeared loyal and steadfast in his strength to move forward after Ryan's death while providing our family financial security.

I, on the other hand, withdrew on weekends for personal private time. I relished in my role as mother during the work week, but once the weekend arrived, I needed privacy to grieve. I found comfort in routine errands, tending to my family as I carefully selected groceries, planned menus, and chose treats as lunch box surprises for the kids to enjoy. I dove into my *Mom* role, but I also found healing shopping on my *Mother's Day Out* as I worked through my pain, often rummaging through racks of children's clothes that reminded me of Ryan. These were my outlets to resume life normally when nothing seemed normal at all without him.

Kyle treated me with kindness and consideration during those times. He never appeared annoyed by my many hours, and sometimes entire weekends, spent away from the house. He understood my need to be alone and seemed comforted by spending time with our kids and their friends.

In my quiet time, I also grew as a new Christian through a BSF (Bible Study Fellowship) evening Bible study. Sometimes I shared my grief, confiding to friends or family when they called. As a couple, we also attended a child bereavement group called Compassionate Friends. However, my alone time was where I found true refuge, comforted from the pain of loss as God whispered in my ear, *"I will never leave or forsake you."*

Immediately following Ryan's death, our trauma was compounded by the sudden deaths of four other family members. In close succession, we also dealt with a lawsuit and wrongful death litigation surrounding the death of Kyle's brother, who suffered from drug and alcohol addiction. Although I missed my husband during his many travels for work and estate business, I understood he needed me as never before. My job was to emotionally support him, trusting he would come home to me in the end.

When his litigations concluded, I recalled fond memories of traveling to South Carolina to spend Easter Sunday with Kyle's mom and her deceased son's only daughter, then eight years old. She beamed with pride as she sang in the church choir, looking down on all of her grandchildren for the very first time due to her elder son's turbulent lifestyle. Two weeks later, she, too, died unexpectedly, with Kyle by her side. The calamities seemed endless and merciless for a family that had already lost so much.

The next year, we built a new home north of Raleigh as we attempted a fresh start toward healing. We could finally build a future without visions of our lost son in each room. However, while Kyle's shell returned from his tragedies physically, it seemed as if I had lost him emotionally to his pain. The dust of repeated trauma began to settle, but the demise of our marriage continued to spiral.

As I enjoyed decorating our new home and making new friends, Kyle was just beginning his journey. His grief walk was unproductive as he carried the burden of anger like a heavy backpack overladen with *Why?* or *How could this happen?* or *I didn't deserve this.* I wanted to comfort him, but he avoided his need for help. This wasn't his style. Instead, we became emotional strangers as he dealt with his grief privately, and our relationship continued to deteriorate.

Our differing stages of grief disrupted the mutual support that had once strengthened our marriage. Kyle's career was his outlet, and his business travels became much more frequent and prolonged. I soon began to look forward to his absences, often preferring them to our time together, which had slowly become more unpleasant and unfulfilling.

As I watched my marriage deteriorate from the pain of unmet needs and emotional abandonment, my emptiness descended into depression, and I became vulnerable to the compassion of another man. A relationship never rooted in this attraction, but I felt a deep sense of accountability due to my commitment to our marriage. Hoping to awaken Kyle to our problems without intentions to hurt him, I confessed to him my feelings for another man. His bitterness and emotional absence was taking a toll on me. I confessed that it felt good to be admired and noticed but that I longed for him alone and the marriage we once knew. I made it clear that I was committed to healing from our many tragedies and expressed my need for him to emotionally return to our relationship.

Kyle immediately scoffed at me, responding that I had grossly misunderstood this mutual attraction.

"Who would want the burden of a married woman with another man's children?"

With calmness and void of emotion, he dismissed me as he turned and walked away.

I was appalled and hurt by his doubt that someone else could find me attractive and desirable. Instead of leading to an open discussion that would help heal us and address our problems, his dismissive attitude and response instead made them even worse.

As Kyle exited the kitchen, I felt degraded by his unloving, uncaring indifference. From then on, our conversations and relationship became increasingly superficial. Outwardly, life appeared to return to business as usual around the house and at work. This conversation became dust beneath the rug, and I found myself fading into the routines of a trapped marriage.

Our two years in our new Raleigh home were stressful, with few good memories to outweigh my sorrow. In 2002, following the tech industry's economic crash, Kyle's job then forced our relocation to Dallas, Texas, igniting the downward spiral of our marriage to its ultimate fate.

Within months of our move to Dallas, my relationship with Kyle went from bad to worse. Holidays and vacations became an emotional strain. Instead of defining a new future with opportunity, it felt as if our lives had become automated by routine. My depression made life without antidepressants inconceivable. I tried to find purpose and healing in this new place, but I felt desperately alone as my husband rapidly became a stranger.

Little did I know that Kyle had already entered a lifestyle of crime, fueled by his secret addiction.

Chapter 3

From Our Beginning

Verse of Reflection

Blessed is the one who trusts in the LORD,
*   whose confidence is in him.*
They will be like a tree planted by the water
*   that sends out its roots by the stream.*
It does not fear when heat comes;
*   its leaves are always green.*
It has no worries in a year of drought
*   and never fails to bear fruit.*

—Jeremiah 17:7-8

*M*any years later, it remains unfathomable to me that our relationship, perfectly imperfect as it was, became tragic virtually overnight. Looking back, I now see that the biggest obstacle toward my healing was my reverence for the past we once knew and my inability to completely let go of the shame.

Kyle and I met at a party in college the week before the onset of classes. I found myself intrigued by this shy, clean-cut, eighteen-year-old ROTC (Reserve Officers Training Corps) student who flirted with me throughout the night. He was sweet and entertaining, plus he had a car. So, I called him the next day and asked if he would escort me and my roommate to shop for a dorm-room rug. He eagerly jumped at the chance. After our shopping trip, he asked me out on a real date.

On our first official date, I was surprised to meet his parents, who'd made an impromptu visit from his hometown in rural eastern South Carolina. They were equally surprised at meeting me so early in our relationship. Over dinner, I got to know Kyle better as his parents proudly filled me in of his many achievements and multiple scholarships. His dad, Fred, leaned over to me and said in his Southern drawl, "I could have kicked his butt when he turned down that Citadel scholarship, but I always told my kids they had to pull their own little red wagon." I immediately loved Fred. He was so much easier to be around than Kyle's mother.

Dinner was pleasant, but after meeting Kyle's folks, I quickly realized that a relationship was unlikely due to our vast cultural differences. I was an upper middle class New York City suburban girl raised by career professionals with advanced college degrees. Kyle was a Southern country boy and former military brat. His father was a retired Air Force sergeant, and his mother grew up on a cotton field with nine brothers and sisters. We knew nothing about each other's worlds. I returned to my dorm with no expectations.

Then, just three weeks into the fall semester, I was diagnosed with mononucleosis. The budding friendships I'd begun at college soon dried up. I was sick and alone. During the long weeks of illness, my excitement about my newfound freedom as a freshman dwindled. I was quarantined by the school physician, and my grades steadily plummeted. My mother pleaded with me to drop out for the semester and return home to New York to recover. However, in my mind, dropping out would signify failure, and so I fought tirelessly to keep up with class demands while my health continued to decline.

Although our relationship was in the beginning stages, Kyle, unlike others, chose not to abandon me. He dedicated his spare time to caring for my needs around his class schedule as I remained in isolation.

The following semester, kidney complications landed me in the hospital during spring break. My mother, opposed to my decision to remain at school, refused to travel when I needed her most. But Kyle voluntarily remained by my side through each health and academic obstacle. He tutored me with compassion and commitment to my success, asking nothing in return. He only wanted to take care of me as no one else would.

We were married four years later after our graduation and his commencement into the Air Force. Three years later we both decided on his early separation from the military. We relocated three times, progressed in our careers, and lived in beautiful homes in nice neighborhoods. We grew closer with the birth of each child and personal achievement. Friends and family referred to us as *the perfect couple* blessed with the perfect life.

Ten years into our marriage, tragedy struck when Ryan died suddenly from a bowel adhesion that took him during the night. Five years earlier, when he was an infant, we had come close to losing him to an intussusception, a medical condition caused when a section of intestine telescopes into an adjacent section causing an obstruction that halts blood flow. With no time to react, the surgeon diagnosed, "This situation is incompatible with life" as he handed me authorization forms before exiting the ER to the operating room to prepare. The emergency surgery saved Ryan's life, and he lived a normal childhood for the five years that followed. We believed we would see him grow up. Instead, we stood blindsided and shocked as we planned his funeral, with no medical explanation and nowhere to turn in our pain.

As weeks passed while we tried to resume our lives, the phone stopped ringing and compassionate visitors dwindled. I was lost. *How do I go on normally without my child?* Emotionally anguished after Ryan's untimely death, I gave my life to God as I fell to my knees on our dining room floor sobbing in grief.

As I began my faith walk as a new Christian, I discovered a transformative peace that brought me a strange comfort as I got through each day, one by one. But Kyle withdrew to a different comforter he secretly harbored. His grief outlet to porn addiction eventually morphed into a criminal lifestyle, sacrificing his reputation, his marriage, his family's future, and, ultimately, his life.

When Kyle and I returned home from Mr. Cavanaugh's office, my mother stood beside the kitchen table, hesitating but eager to inquire about the results of our meeting.

"Did everything go well?" she asked.

My husband quietly proceeded to the bedroom to pack.

"Kyle will be leaving us today. I'll fill you in afterward," I replied sadly.

Soon afterward, my best friend and lifetime love walked out the door and drove away in his truck.

My head hurt from all I'd come to learn that day. I sat beside my mother on the sofa, laid my head on her soft chest, and sobbed like a child as my heart broke. I knew she ached also as I felt her tears fall onto my head. Never in my adult life had I needed her nurturing and empathy as much as at that moment. I was not thinking about what would happen next.

Instead, I could only feel the pain of watching my husband, now a stranger, walk out that door, soon to become a felon.

There would be no reconciliation with the man I saw transformed by addiction that day. I did not know him, nor did I want to know him. He was no longer trustworthy. Therefore, I had to separate from him and shield myself and our children from his exposed life of crime and duality. From that point on, my primary responsibility was to my children as a single parent. Not knowing if I would ever see him again, I fell into my mother's arms and sobbed as if this goodbye was Kyle's funeral. However, this was worse. He was not dead. He was still alive and would remain to haunt me.

After my mother returned to her home in New York a few days later, she called often to check on me. During our conversations, I could tell she'd been crying. Due to her progressive mental decline, she repeatedly revisited that dark day my husband left. She asked the same questions, over and over, each time we spoke. As I explained what happened, her heart broke as she relived each incident. She loved Kyle as a son and was proud of our union.

A few months passed following our separation and my immediate filing for divorce. Kyle had moved to an extended stay motel while seeking new employment as he awaited the criminal charges soon to be filed against him. His lawyer advised him not to leave Dallas as the FBI concluded their investigation of his computer evidence.

One afternoon after the kids arrived home from school, he called. I exited the kitchen back door as I picked up the phone to shield them from overhearing their father's repeated harassments.

"What is it now, Kyle?" I asked with annoyance in my tone.

"You need to stop the divorce now," Kyle answered. "You're destroying our family. You know I'm not guilty of anything. I didn't touch anyone."

"Really? You touched no one?" I sneered with sarcasm as I

recalled his confessions in Mr. Cavanaugh's office. I tried not to visualize the many prostitutes he'd engaged with, but images kept popping into my head.

As Kyle continued to point blame at me, I wondered how the man I once loved had become so twisted. His perception of reality was skewed, and he'd begun believing the lies he told with reluctance to accept any wrongdoing.

Just how far would he take this, I wondered.

He continued with the true purpose for his call. "I've taken a job in Tucson, Arizona. I want you and the kids to go with me. We are a family, and that doesn't need to change. We can be a family anywhere. No one will know about this. They won't find us there. Stop all this now and come with me."

How dependent and shallow does he think I am? Will he ever accept the loss of my support and admit to his lies?

Knowing this was another desperate attempt to pull at my heartstrings, I calmly responded to Kyle's confident persuasion.

"Kyle, you have a problem and need help. Pay the fine and stay in Dallas," I said. "If you do the right thing and get help, I won't divorce you. I'll stay with you, and we'll continue to work things out," I bargained, hoping he would finally awaken to accept the severity of his crimes.

"I don't have a problem," he said.

"Well, then, I do," I answered and ended the call.

At that moment, I went into survivor mode, and reality set in that it was paramount to cut ties. Our safety and financial security were now gone. Steadfast to protect what remained of my family, I refused future calls from my husband and proceeded with the divorce.

Kyle began life as a fugitive as he accepted the new job in Tucson, Arizona. His goal was to escape conviction of federal charges, including possession and solicitation of child pornography. Gripping onto his innocence, he refused the plea bargain offered by the district attorney as he fled Texas.

Kyle Visited Me in My Dreams

My Kyle came to see me in my dreams this morning. I had trouble sleeping all night. I consumed half a bottle of wine before bed and decided not to risk taking a sleeping pill but instead, to try to sleep on my own. I'd not slept well since you left, but I was so tired. I thought, maybe I'll sleep tonight without a pill. I really should try.

It's been over two months now since you left. I was up most of the night, able only to rest slightly. Around five in the morning, lightning flashed. Our lab, Shadow, immediately became anxious, and I dragged myself out of bed to the kitchen to get her medication as she started reacting to the oncoming thunderstorm. I quickly walked her outside in the dark, gave her a pill, and hoped she'd soon settle down. I fell back into bed and finally drifted off to sleep.

And then I saw you walking around to my bedside to sit down and kiss me goodbye before work, as you did every day for twenty years. You were dressed in a blue shirt, jeans, and the same aged blue military belt you never would replace. You had an airline ticket in your right hand. It was obvious you were about to travel somewhere that morning for work. As you lowered your face toward mine, you looked at me with those soft green eyes and that look of adoration that always sucked me in helplessly. Your look was indisputable. You loved me. It was that simple.

Your clean-shaven cheeks revealed every pore of your face. I could smell your aftershave. I wanted to be closer to you before you left, and I hated to see you go. I poured on the seductress to tempt you before you left. You smiled at the possibility, and I hoped you'd next untie my robe. You were my officer and a gentleman, so confident and whole. For some reason, you loved me. Any woman would be lucky to have you, but you chose me. I basked in your love and protection as no place I'd rather be.

Then the alarm went off. I flashed back to the present as I awoke suddenly, and you were gone. I went upstairs to get our youngest son ready for school while looking forward to returning home to bed to meet you again in my dreams. But you never came. I was alone, left behind, wishing you'd come home. Now, I accepted there would never be a homecoming. My Kyle was gone permanently, replaced by someone I didn't know, like, or respect. Grief then accompanied a tidal wave of memories as I longed for the man who'd left my bedside that morning.

I remember loving how you spooned next to me as I slept, purposely putting your arm around my pregnant belly to feel our first son grow and move within me. I remember you twirling me with glee when I hung up the phone with the doctor's news of the pregnancy test results. In the delivery room months later, I also remember you chomping on popcorn as I sucked on ice chips, while we watched endless news reports of the Persian Gulf crisis that preceded my labor that day.

And then, I remember the man who stood brave and righteous before so many people just five years later at our son's funeral. Even though your heart was broken, you courageously stood next to Ryan's little coffin, holding our youngest son, Grayson, in your arms, and spoke your eulogy of the child's life well lived. I don't even remember exactly what you said, but only how much I admired and loved you. This was the man I married, and I was so proud to call you mine.

I remember loving how you loved me, how you cared for me in college when I was so sick, and how you always covered me with a blanket when I fell asleep on the sofa. I remember the candlelight dinners at Chez Kyle's and all the spontaneous meals you prepared throughout our marriage, awaiting me with a glass of wine.

I remember how you yearned for me and how we craved each other after only a week apart during a school break. And lastly, after I resolved that our marriage was over after losing our son, I remember the roses and balloons awaiting me when I visited the graveyard following a huge fight. Oh, how I always came back to you.

But now, I could no longer come back again. This person who now possesses you is not my Kyle, and to return to our marriage would be emotional suicide. Your pain changed you and led you to an addiction that robbed me of my marriage and you of your reputation, self-respect, and, most importantly, your children. My Kyle, everyone's perfect Kyle, was gone, lost in battle, Satan's victory for your soul. All I can do now is pray for your healing as I treasure our memories, wishing this new reality was instead a bad dream, and earnestly hope you'll eventually return to the man I once loved.

Chapter 4

From His Addiction's Beginning

Verse of Reflection

Do not be misled: "Bad company corrupts good character." Come back to your senses as you ought, and stop sinning; for there are some who are ignorant of God—I say this to your shame.

—1 Corinthians 15:33–34

With each passing day, I struggled to keep moving forward, disillusioned by how I had come to this place. I still fought to accept Dallas as our new home, and my existence revolved around loneliness. Our house changed from a home filled with comforts, family, and new friendships to a new survival project filled with choices and decisions. I was overcome by the darkness of my present, the uncertainties of my future, and the abyss of addiction's consequences.

I continually tried to determine at what point Kyle had exchanged his love for me for the lusts of underage girls and paid women, both online and offline. How long had my life been a mere illusion where my officer and gentleman was nothing more than a fictional character in my ideal world as the perfect couple with the perfect life? Was his love for me ever authentic and real? If so, when and how did it convert to a double lifestyle born of his unmet needs?

As I sat and listened to his confessions that day in his lawyer's office, my world suddenly became surreal. I was angered by his camouflage of lies, realizing how he had used gaslighting and mental manipulation against me for so many years to dismiss my instinct that something was off and very wrong with his behavior.

Despite my anger and confusion, my heart still hurt for my husband daily as I struggled to build a new life without him. While my primary task was to provide financial security after years as a stay-at-home mom, I often lacked intention and focus. I fell victim to an emotional haze of fog and despair, longing for Kyle's presence and voice. However, I knew I could not see or speak to him, as any contact would spark a cycle of codependency that would fuel arguments and more animosity.

So instead, one morning after dropping the kids off at school, I sat at the kitchen table in sweatpants and a cap and began writing letters to Kyle in the months and years that followed. Heartfelt thoughts poured onto the notepad as tears dripped onto each page. With no intention to share these thoughts with him, I downloaded my pain in pen and ink journaling my grief walk, thereby releasing me mentally to get on with my day.

As I emotionally processed all that had happened, I folded each letter and hid it away in our safe. I put one foot in front of the other daily as I took baby steps toward healing. My only solace was my role as a mom with the responsibilities and routines of parenthood to keep me on course.

During that time, I was also driven to understand the psychology and progression of sexual addiction, educating myself of the growing yet unpublicized phenomenon that had suddenly entered my world. I searched online and scoured libraries and bookstores to gain knowledge about sexual addiction and available treatments. I craved information, desperately needing to comprehend how Kyle could conceal his addiction from all of his relationships for so long. In my quest to find answers to my many questions about addiction's transformations, I learned of its progressive cycle, the fuel of underlying emotional pain, the multiplication of symptoms, and the narcissism it births to mask its degenerative behaviors from others.

Knowledge slowly replaced disillusionment with a sense of compassion as I mentally envisioned the pains that haunted Kyle, tempting his slow surrender to addiction as he frequented relief from his new outlet of pornography. Over time, his temptations grew more alluring, meeting his need for unconditional love on demand to soothe his sadness. As he spiraled into addiction's cycle, his self-worth deteriorated and morphed into a mental illness that rationalized his negative behaviors. He fell helpless to his addiction's insatiable, compulsive desires for comfort and gratification, eventually presenting danger to his family and personal lifestyle as addiction's appetite demanded a more intense satisfaction at any cost.

My research gave me new insight on the marital challenges we had faced these past years, preventing our marriage from healing after Ryan's death. I realized the first evidence was his long-lived withdrawn interest in our physical relationship, which had drastically degenerated for ten years since the loss of our son. I was more supportive than alarmed by his disinterest, respecting his need to process this tragedy privately. Through my pardons and excuses, I failed to acknowledge his disinterest as a sign of a problem far deeper.

While researching, I combed my mind for behaviors that may have shown signs of Kyle's addiction, and flashbacks of memories came rushing back to me.

One evening, I found a prescription bottle of Viagra in the laundry basket. "What's this for?" I asked as I held up the bottle to him.

Kyle replied matter-of-factly, "The doctor prescribed them. We both know I have high blood pressure, and it affects my performance."

"What performance?" I answered sarcastically, diving further toward an explanation.

"You lost interest years ago! What I don't understand is why that doesn't bother you. So why would you go to the doctor without talking to me first?"

Kyle dismissed my question and walked away. Angered, I flushed the pills down the toilet. When he heard this, he rushed back to the bathroom.

"What have you done? Do you have any idea what that cost?" he scolded.

But he neglected to see the high cost of the intimacy that had been lost in our relationship and refused to acknowledge my hurt and frustration. As I revisited that moment now armed with knowledge, I could later surmise that his prescription instead served to prolong his satisfaction during engagements with his paid partners.

I continued to recall additional memories that served as red flags and unveiled new discoveries in the war against our marriage.

I began to suspect infidelity with Kyle's lack of desire and remote phone calls in various parts of the house. Committed to our relationship, I presented him with an olive branch versus ending the marriage then. "If you have someone else, get rid of her now, and I'll ask no questions."

He arrogantly scoffed at my suspicions. "There's no one but you," Kyle replied, dismissing my concerns and feelings as he walked out of the room.

He became narcissistic, rationalizing my doubts and purposely eroding my confidence as he turned my questions into my personal paranoia. During his mind games, he remained steadfast as he dismissed and justified his peculiar behaviors. I was left confused and depressed, but my instincts were relentless that something was very wrong. *Was I becoming emotionally off balance?*

His twisted promises and "I love you"s were further diluted when I walked into the bedroom one Saturday morning to find him alone in a compromising position. I was astonished and hurt, ripped of my womanhood by his illusion of sex acts with an imaginary mistress.

"We'll discuss this later tonight after the kids go to bed," I responded as I exited the bedroom.

Later that evening, our scheduled conversation behind closed bedroom doors became a heated argument. As I folded laundry on the bed, I began by calmly asking him why he felt inclined to exchange my willingness and desire for a mere imagery with someone else.

"You said there was no one else, and that you loved me."

Without remorse or apology, he smugly claimed he preferred his imagery to me.

Our discussion then escalated to extremes. I became

infuriated and spontaneously reached for a pillow to defend my womanhood. I hit Kyle repeatedly with my weapon while angrily responding in a firm but soft voice so as not to wake the kids.

"*How dare you!* Get out of this house now because we will not be sharing a roof tonight."

He turned and walked away toward the garage as if to leave, and I was relieved.

As my anger subsided, I took a deep breath.

Minutes later, the McKinney police arrived at our home. I answered the door and was greeted by two officers.

"Ma'am, please exit the house."

"What's going on?" I asked.

"Your husband called to report a domestic violence incident," the policeman said. "Can you tell us what happened?"

At that moment, I saw my husband present himself from the garage wearing retribution all over his face. I was astounded and utterly embarrassed to answer the officer's question.

I looked down in shame, forced to explain what happened. I could see them each trying to restrain their laughter.

"All right, if your spouse is pressing charges for domestic violence, you'll need to leave the house and come with us," the officer said.

"What? Are you kidding me! After what he said to me?" I argued.

"Yes, one of you needs to leave tonight."

He turned toward Kyle. "Sir, will you be pressing charges?"

With a smirk on his face, Kyle finally spoke up, savoring my humiliation.

"I won't press charges. You can stay, but only for the kids' sake," he replied, positioning himself as the hero. He grinned at me spitefully in vengeance as he opened the door to his truck, and he left.

As we tried to move past these trials to build a life in Dallas, our beautiful new home had become my cage. I tried to commit to working through our problems but continued to struggle as I fell into a deep sadness. Eventually, I sought professional counseling to make sense of the craziness.

I recall sharing with my counselor how I felt trapped in my sadness, unable to experience real joy of any kind, no matter how intentionally I tried.

"I'm trying so hard to make our house a home. I have twelve colors of green sampled on my wall, and I can't *feel* any of them," I explained.

"What do you mean by *feel*?" my counselor asked.

"The walls and trims in my home are beige. I've been trying desperately to make our home *feel* cozy, but nothing soothes me or brings me happiness. I can't *feel* any of them. Normally, a color inspires a mood of comfort or fun, but all I feel is helpless. It's as if I can't find the perfect color to heal my sadness."

The counselor compassionately smiled at me in response. "When people are depressed, they often lose their natural sense of smell or taste. You've lost a different sense as a creative type, and that's your natural sense to *feel* color," she explained.

Her diagnosis provided me with temporary relief. I no longer felt crazy, but my quest for normal created an inner battle for happiness that progressively eroded my spirit.

Living with Kyle's hidden addiction continued my struggles with what was real and what was not. I had a loving husband, a beautiful home, and our children had a great father. We were financially secure, and I was fortunate to be a stay-at-home mom to raise our kids while caring long-distance for an elderly parent. This was the life I signed up for after recommitting to our marriage prior to our relocation to Dallas.

But the days Kyle looked at me with adoration were replaced with indifference I couldn't translate. Occasionally, I'd see glimpses of the man I fell in love with. Some days, he would arrive home with flowers while at other times, he was a stranger to me. His inconsistent behavior transformed his gestures of love to empty affections.

But one thing never changed: the predictable kiss he always prioritized before departing for work each day, even when we disagreed. I depended on him for that kiss before he left to assure me we were still okay. How foolish I now felt, thinking back on those empty kisses and promises.

After the police visit, confrontations, denial, and confusion, my marriage now entrapped me in a beautiful home filled with sorrow and self-doubt. After months of running on emotional fumes, I broke down one evening in sadness. I fell to the floor in our master bedroom closet and wept uncontrollably for two hours. With hot tears running down my cheeks, I looked up at my beautiful collection of lingerie hanging in the closet and grieved as my marriage slowly dissolved. In my pain and frustration, I responded with a pair of scissors, shredding each gown regardless of its cost, and continued to sob in the debris of satin and lace. The closet doors opened, and I saw Kyle standing there peering down at me. "Are you done yet?" he asked coldly. "You're upsetting the children."

At that moment, I knew our marriage was over. Kyle's disrespect depicted a man I no longer recognized. I realized that my purpose as his wife had become limited to tending to our house and raising our children. I took action the next day and proceeded with efforts to separate and divorce.

After I'd filed for divorce, signed a lease, and scheduled movers, Kyle successfully coerced me to stay with his sly persuasions, and I melted under his spell one last time. As I packed and prepared for the next day's move, he greeted me with pizza for the kids and reservations at my favorite restaurant. His final manipulation choreographed aged steaks and wine with a promise to dedicate himself to marriage counseling if I'd suspend the divorce proceedings.

Despite our individual and couple's counseling during

the next six months, my hollowness grew deeper. His plot of narcissism thickened, using his innate charisma to fool me and our trained counselors. In the end, I later learned he scheduled our counseling sessions to coincide with his hooker adulteries beforehand just blocks away.

From the desk of Kathryn Lackey . . .

The Months that Followed

The weeks and months passed away, leaving tread marks on our family due to the indiscretions of just one. The self-destruction of a successful career, a loving family and marriage rippled sadness to friends, coworkers, and family members astonished by the sins of one so close. The accused once masked the facade of accomplishment but now openly revealed a sex offender and a child predator none of us would have ever suspected.

It was often hard to believe that the sex addict suffered any more than his spouse and children. He failed to accept and comprehend the harsh sentence that was to follow as he continued to justify his innocence. We would each then face our individual prisons as we moved forward with life following a jury's judgment, trying to release ourselves from our family's shame.

"I didn't touch anyone. I harmed no one physically. Others have done far worse than me," he justified in his defense. Although he admitted to a mistake that bruised his trustworthiness, his sin fogged his comprehension of the severity of what he had done, the personal consequences of a pending divorce and supervised visitation. Lastly, it blinded him of the hardship he was about to endure in prison for his perverted attraction to over 2,200 innocent young female children of parents just like us.

Each day as I awakened, I was hit by a fresh wave of grief and a piercing gravity of the consequences to our family. We had entered *a harrowing reality of lawyers, divorce, court trials, and inevitably, my husband's prison sentence.*

With my circumstances often unbearable, I refused to succumb to chronic depression. Holidays, birthdays, and anniversaries challenged my ability to survive their emotional tidal waves. Solitary weekends, dinner hours, and the sight of his empty chair felt like treading water tirelessly in an ocean of grief. Each day, I'd gather the strength to pull myself out of the water, some days with more energy than others.

Sometimes, I would field inquiries from friends who'd say, "You are doing so well for what you've been through." They didn't realize that my faith in God kept me steady through the typhoon of emotional waves. Our lives were now irreversibly changed.

My husband's prison sentence affected us all with the consequences of his continued defiance and unrepentance. I grieved for my marriage and family life as it once was but knew it could never be restored. I was forced to let go and clung to God's promises, knowing He would deliver me and our children to a new life awaiting us on the other side of the pain.

Bleeding and broken, I hung by only a thread of grace. I had to believe God would walk me through the destruction of our beautiful life and restore me to higher ground, for without that belief, I had nothing.

Chapter 5

A Final Parting

Verse of Reflection

For in the day of trouble
he will keep me safe in his dwelling;
he will hide me in the shelter of his sacred tent
and set me high upon a rock.

—Psalm 27:5

*M*y new reality as a single parent began, and divorce proceedings resumed. Automations of school, sports, and household chores provided a welcome distraction from the pain and heartache looming in the shadows of each new day.

There was so much to plan, a future unknown. *Where would we live, when would we move, and how would I support us?* Overwhelm continually threatened my sound decisions. My children's provision and healing became a catalyst, focusing me to push through the fog to reconstruction. This new season began with a commitment to our recovery during a market downturn and an elderly parent's needs. I was alone and afraid, but time was not my friend. I was forced to reinvent myself promptly following one of the worst tragedies of my life.

During this time, while I worked through decisions for our future, Kyle clung to his innocence pending a forthcoming indictment. While the FBI continued to gain evidence from his confiscated work computer, he accepted a job in Tucson, Arizona, ignoring his lawyer's advice to remain in Texas and accept a plea bargain versus the risk of potential prison consequences.

Up until this point, my communication with Kyle had been very limited. However, I still longed for his presence, the soothing sound of his voice, and the comfort they once offered. It was a daily struggle not to daydream about a past filled with happiness, then suddenly replaced by the pain of destruction. Though Kyle was gone, my love for him was not. I cried each night in the darkness, emotionally exhausted from visions of his infidelities as I attempted to sleep. The cycle would continue as the sun rose on yet another day and my new reality.

One afternoon after my children returned home from school, I busied myself upstairs. I glanced up and saw Kyle's truck driving toward the house through the window of our study. My heart jumped. Fear wrestled with my excitement at seeing him once again. I remained upstairs as he rang the doorbell. Our son answered the door. I eavesdropped as Kyle entered the house. Taking a deep breath, I then walked downstairs to ensure our son's safety.

"What are you doing here?" I asked calmly.

"I'm dropping off Grayson's bike pump," Kyle replied, strangely avoiding eye contact.

"I thought he would need it. I'm leaving for Arizona tomorrow."

As I studied him, Kyle's evasiveness made me feel guarded. I doubted his explanation was the true purpose for his visit but instead a mere excuse to say goodbye to the kids without acknowledging the court's visitation requirements. His disrespect for authority persevered.

My fleeting secret joy at seeing my husband again diminished as I looked closer at him. Something was off. His eyes were bloodshot, and his gate unsteady. The man standing at my door was someone I no longer knew or trusted and a mere shell of my husband. His soul was now gone. I stood cautioned, suspecting possible drug use, and peacefully escorted him back to his truck.

The following day was the first of many to come, where Kyle and I would begin our separate lives far away from each other as he headed off to Tucson. I'd just returned home from taking our son to school, finding Kyle parked at the curb. I drove into the garage and remained silent as I slowly approached his truck.

Kyle kept his gaze fixed on the windshield. "I came to say goodbye," he said, his tone flat, void of any remorse.

I fought back the tears as my heart broke with the reality of that moment. I wanted to say "Don't go" or "Let me go with you" and return to our past lives when we were happy and our family was whole. However, deep in my soul, I knew Kyle had changed and was no longer a man I trusted. Our past memories held the man I once loved in a time capsule and family photo albums.

His visit was short, and the conversation was limited. Neither of us had words left to say. Together half our lives, we parted at the crossroads of his new life on the run.

The following Sunday was my birthday, the first of many without Kyle. Once upon a time, I had looked forward to it as he typically spoiled me. Now, I dreaded the day, instead filled with a deep sadness. I felt so alone. Despite my children's attempts to make me feel special with a fully dressed dining room table set for a celebration dinner, I moped most of the day.

Fighting fatigue and emotional burden, I headed to church, hoping God would inspire me with a message specifically targeted to me. I continually wrestled with my heart's desire to remain a family. And then, as I absorbed the pastor's delivery that morning, God faithfully spoke to that desire, awakening me to His message of restoration and hope.

I sensed God, much like a father who comforts his crying child, wrapping me with His shawl of protection as my world shattered. I found myself propelled back to the time Ryan died, when I first sensed God's presence as I lay sobbing on our dining room floor. He provided me purpose to resist taking my own life through my love for Kyle and my two remaining children. God showed me that He still had a plan for my life, even though my child's life had ended suddenly and without reason. He would provide his strength through my faith and guide my family toward healing. But His love for Kyle was even greater than mine, and I had to let go and trust God to bring him to a place of submission in order to finally redeem him from his addiction.

Despite my great sorrow and pain from Kyle's betrayals, I loved the person behind the addiction the way he once was so many years before. I also longed for his deliverance as I watched his illness cast aside good judgments. As he spiraled out of control, I relinquished control and trusted that, with time, God would guide my husband down a path of redemption and lay for him a new foundation of purpose, brick by brick. My heart resolved that this was His journey with Kyle, a walk necessary to ultimately heal and reconcile his pain. The choice to accept help was Kyle's alone. I chose to step back, refocus on myself and our children, and trust that God was now in control of both our futures.

Letter of Goodbye

⸎

Dear Kyle,

My emotions these days are like landmines. The days and times of explosions are erratic, each ignited by the trauma of what you've done. Writing this letter is my way of relieving my pain and letting you know that my anguish continually overflows with its roots anchored in the depths of my love.

For many years, I have known that our marriage was less than perfect. Our relationship and intimate connection degenerated steadily, leaving me mystified and frustrated. Our lives became automated, and slowly, our closeness evaporated. I confess my self-image withered behind your mask of devotion, repeatedly falling victim to your mockings and rejections. "Of course, I love you," you would respond as you rationalized and cast aside my questions, leaving me despondent and often belittled.

Left feeling hollow, I remained patient and focused my heartache to other tasks. Your disregard for my need to rebuild a once solid marriage steadily eroded my confidence as I witnessed your character's subtle changes. While other parents have lost children and survived the tragedy, their relationships healed and often grew closer. Why couldn't ours?

Now, I ramble around in this house day after day, still numb from my disbelief at the pain you've inflicted on yourself and this family. I thirst for books on sexual addiction to understand your *new comforter, the culprit that sacrificed our present and future. Knowledge is my bridge to understanding your struggle and the inner pain that wrestled your soul to a bottomless darkness.*

In turn, I realize my own codependency and ways I unknowingly contributed to your addiction cycles. When I should have set boundaries, instead my trust and compassion enabled you with ample excuses for your need to grieve, given our loss. I wanted our life together so very much, and I passionately believed God would eventually bring us healing as a couple. Your choices, however, prevented His intervention with your desires focused on your repeated needs for forbidden flesh.

While I knew work on our marriage would remain a constant dedication between us, I never wavered in my trust of your love for me and the kids. I respected and admired you for all you had endured and overcome. Life had not been fair, but you stood boldly dedicated to your family despite all of your adversities.

Now, the truth of your double life has been revealed, and you are gone. You became an impersonator of the man we all believed you to be, allowing your lies to transform you. My love and recommitment to you blinded me from the double life you'd created from your pain. While I patiently longed for you to need and desire me all these years, your needs were met by the skills of hookers, eventually becoming your secret obsession. You became a consumer of superficial pleasure in exchange for money. How empty and used you must have felt, fondled by women as a mere object, void of the respect and love I offered to you unconditionally.

In contrast, I saw the person beneath the skin, the man I believed also loved me. All these years, my desire was to become your trusted source of comfort. I longed for you to rediscover the goodness of us, but you drifted further and further away. In my despair and ignorance of addiction's cancer growing within you, I failed to draw you back home to our relationship where you belonged.

Now, I face my life without you. I am without a husband, soon to be divorced, and my children are without a father. You no longer serve as a positive influence or role model. You have risked all that we have for a life of deceit and immorality. As often as I want to forgive you and reconstruct our shattered lives, I realize the man I once loved is now gone. Only your shell remains. You are not the person I married. You are a sick man I do not know, one filled with great pain who has ignored the healing power of his family's love. It would be unfair to our kids to keep hoping and praying for a future together. If you are unwilling to recover from your addiction, your disregard for our safety makes the risk too great. I want our children to grow up in a family modeled with love, not pain and sadness. Our daughter will be going off to college in five years. As I step away and heal, I have limited time to repair the past and reinvent goodness within our family for her.

I will continue to pray for your recovery during our lives apart. For those prayers to be answered, you must first let go of the pain and admit you need help from God and others familiar with this same addiction.

I want you to know I once loved you and am truly sorry for any pain I've caused you. However, you and I had the opportunity to overcome tragedy and recreate a wonderful future together. It was your choice to mask your pain secretly until it overflowed uncontrollably causing calamity to our lives. Now, I will refocus my love for you solely on the kids, realizing they are my primary purpose.

Kathy

Chapter 6

The Power of Knowledge

Verse of Reflection

I am sending you out like sheep among wolves. Therefore be as shrewd as snakes and as innocent as doves.

—Matthew 10:16

*M*y life with Kyle was now over. I was left hollow and unprepared for *what's next*, knowing my first defense was to understand the atrocities that had entered our lives as I processed the traumas of the past few months.

As his truck faded from view, Kyle was gone at last. A new life in Arizona awaited him as he left his family and his crimes behind. His indictment loomed behind our divorce process, with each case prolonged and wearisome during the months that followed.

I don't know which event leading to this point stripped my soul more. As I watched Kyle drive away for the last time, my heart ached for our family the way we once were before the death of our son ten years prior. I unknowingly watched the man I loved turn to a secret comforter that would forever change him into someone I no longer knew. Our world was suddenly shattered, and the memories of our past would never join the dreams for our future. I now found myself forced to relinquish Kyle to his consequences as he drove away, choosing to flee from a pending indictment for a new life on the run.

Disillusioned by months of drama, I turned to go inside the house, stopping briefly to gaze and reflect on the brick facade that once hid the secrets of an unknown sex offender. Neighbors watched as my husband's sex crimes extinguished a family's picture-perfect life. I was left a victim of his scandals, ostracized and isolated by the judgments of others, with our reputations publicly tarnished by gossip and shame.

Now as Kyle embarked on a new life, I realized I was finally released from the chokehold of trauma to build a new future amid the ashes of his destruction. Numb to a future of unknowns, I repeated the question in my mind, *What should I do now?*

Walking back into the house, I headed to the kitchen and collapsed in a chair at the table. With my head in my hands, I gave myself the grace to cry for all I'd been through and the many decisions that lay ahead. Wiping the tears from my eyes, I knew my children's stability depended on my choice to heal, and every decision would impact their precious childhood and future lives. The enormity of responsibility was overwhelming. Only one thing, however, was clear. I could not heal until I understood how my husband changed from a devoted husband and father to a sexual deviant who destroyed our family's life.

Step One—Shedding the Role of Victim

As I sat at the kitchen table, survival replaced shock as the next level of my grief. Overwhelmed by fog, disillusionment, and sorrow, I felt defeated before I'd even begun to rebuild. Yet, I knew I wanted a life for my family free of victimization from my husband's actions. Survival was my immediate instinct, but a life untainted by shame was my goal.

Finally unleashed to make plans for my family's future, I realized that fear presented my biggest obstacle and barrier to my progress. It was first necessary to define that fear to destroy its compounding strength. So I asked myself what I was most afraid of, then positioned my mindset on strategies to conquer its power of intimidation toward failure. This required that I shed my role as Kyle's victim and discover a bold confidence in myself as I claimed my future and my *WHY*. This fundamental goal would provide focus and intention toward a solid future when my initiatives risked a contrasting life of day-to-day survival. Only then could I make clear decisions toward recovery and protect my family from my husband who had now become a fugitive controlled by his addictive instincts.

Over the next several months, I intentionally turned from depression daily, with all its anxiety and antidepressants, as I committed to healing and focused on my mental transition in my new role as a single mom. I recognized that emotional burdens could easily weigh me down and leave me feeling hopeless in my situation, so I first identified and prioritized positive steps *within* my control as I set aside negative mindsets. My goal was to develop a vision toward my future and an action plan to recover and rebuild from my trauma. No one was coming to rescue me, and I realized that mindset and self-care was paramount to gaining strength for the journey ahead.

After driving the kids to school, I began each day with a physical and emotional exercise routine that included three-mile-long prayer walks with the dog. This enabled me to think and talk with God, trusting Him to lead me through the struggles of building a new life on my own.

I was encouraged by trusted family and friend relationships that supported me throughout my healing. I also continued mental health counseling and attended Christian support groups. This helped me sort through the fears and confusion threatening my sound judgments. Addiction-related support groups, including Celebrate Recovery and COSA (Codependents of Sex Addicts), introduced me to new understandings of addiction to strongholds including food, substances, and their related codependent behaviors. I also discovered a compassion for others investing in their own healing within these communities and dedicated to recovery from addiction's compulsive cycles.

In COSA specifically, I met many other wives, including a pastor's wife. Some were still married, and some were not. Not one woman in that room was spared the question, "Can this marriage be saved?" One shared her therapist's advice to write "trust" on a piece of toilet paper, then flush it as her partner's risk replaced her trust. Could she remain in a marriage that fostered such risk? The wives who decided to remain in their marriages and share in their husband's recoveries were encouraged by their spouse's dedication to a twelve-step recovery program.

However, any unfaithfulness and addictive behaviors were treated with boundaries and severe consequences.

While I felt compassion, I also felt shame, unable to contribute support to the emotions of other wives who were also hurting. When I could barely help myself, their stories spiraled my PTSD to even greater depths of sorrow and despair. I then knew with conviction that I wanted to understand my husband's addiction so I could comprehend his mindset in harboring such crimes. However, I also knew that I deserved better in marriage than to accept a spouse based on conditions.

I also attended DivorceCare, where I made the first positive step toward my mental self-care. God walked with me and guided me toward healing, but He also provided a resource of a different kind. As I look back, I truly believe there are no coincidences with God. I later learned that He had a plan all along to introduce me to someone in that class who would become instrumental in guiding me to protection on the next legal maze of my journey.

As I slowly learned to put one foot in front of the other, I heard God's whisper on my heart as He guided me on my path to healing, *Follow Me, and let Me reveal the person of strength I made you to be.* I felt peace as He revealed I must first grieve the death of my identity as a wife to unveil my individual value apart from my marriage. As I peeled back the layers of anger, rejection, and shame, I discovered a new confidence and inner strength to comprehend the complexities of my husband's sexual addiction without malice or personal shame.

I stopped in a Christian bookstore one afternoon, again driving my own healing through resources on addiction recovery for spouses. But God faithfully guided me to a soft-covered workbook on divorce instead. *I will give you rest and healing*, I heard God whisper quietly as I removed the book from its shelf. This book became my lifeline and close friend as we explored nuggets of healing reflections each night, relaxing by the fire.

Step Two—The Power of Knowledge

In addition to my faith, my greatest empowerment through self-discovery was identifying knowledge as my key to healing and the transformative power of my forgiveness.

I dressed my night table with volumes of books from the local library and Amazon. At night after the kids were asleep, each book enlightened me to addiction's powerful force of progression. Through my research, I was slowly able to replace anger with understanding and compassion for my husband, who fell into mental illness as well as temptation.

Strangely, I also recognized the intense inner conflicts caused by pain that sparked Kyle's addictive behaviors. Even though I was unsure if these emotions were rooted in our son's death or a culmination of multiple family losses, his choice to avoid his pain through distractions of online pornography evolved into a force of temptation he could no longer control. Secretly frequenting his comforter regularly, he became empowered toward risk, intensifying his dopamine reward. He grew dependent on this gratification. As his dependence grew stronger, he manifested deceit to hide his activities from family and coworkers, voluntarily defying his ethics as his addiction progressed toward experimentation.

My comprehension of the driving force behind the addiction cycle helped me understand the mental illness that robbed my husband's soul. As I entered his secret darkness, I was able to shed the shame of the temptations that gripped him and release myself as its victim.

Step Three—Gaining Insight

My research also enlightened me to addiction's behavioral patterns, and I began to understand the progression of his addiction in the shadows of our daily lives. This new knowledge enabled me to begin separating myself from my husband's illness and recognize my gift of discernment when instinct repeatedly alarmed me of an undisclosed problem. As I read each resource, I was reminded of the dual personalities of Dr. Jekyll and Mr. Hyde. Mr. Hyde was untamable, controlling Dr. Jekyll's temptations so he could surface more frequently. Hyde lived a reality of evil creation, and his destruction of Jekyll's values invited further destruction as his power over him grew progressively stronger.

In a similar way, I knew Kyle, the man I married, very well. However, I feared his pseudo-counterpart, the other Kyle, a personality that used his innocence to mask his evil intentions, regardless of the consequences to himself and others. As he succumbed to temptation's power and hid his negative behaviors from the outside world, his addiction fueled his ego and empowered him toward risk. He became blind to danger, and his only goal was refuge and soothing from the temptations that haunted him, caused by deep conflicts within.

Stages of Sexual Addiction

In his book *Out of the Shadows*, Dr. Patrick Carnes provided me insight with his clear descriptions of each phase of addiction and its progression:

1. *Preoccupation*—the addict's mind is continually distracted by sex-related thoughts, and he is left vulnerable to temptations as he secretly longs for sexual stimulation.
2. *Ritualization*—the addict creates a time-and-place routine when he can reward his sexual compulsions anonymously. His new rituals add to his arousal and excitement as he plots and fantasizes his next encounter.

3. *Compulsive sexual behavior*—the addict loses his ability to control his desires. He rationalizes each reward as his addiction craves gratification, preoccupying his thoughts and progressing to the next stage.

4. *Despair*—the addict's self-esteem erodes as he finds himself powerless to control the repeated cycles of his compulsive behavior. Conflicting with his inner shame, he masks his actions from the awareness of others, and surrenders to the desires that continually haunt and tempt him.

A Walk Through the Mind of a Sexual Addict

Phase I—Preoccupation

Sexual addiction begins when feelings of unworthiness or trauma meet with experimental engagement. In my quest to understand my husband's mindset toward change, I began to tour his fantasy. I met the addict, a man I knew to be Kyle, unconsciously controlled by his inner pain, comforted in isolation by the unconditional love-on-demand of cybersex porn. With growing anticipation for their next time together, he created more frequent opportunities to isolate himself with his online comforter, rewarded by dopamine. His resistance to temptation deteriorated, and his preoccupation grew into an obsession to plan their secret rendezvous. His resulting shame forced him to mask his new addiction from others, distracting his focus at home and at work.

Phase II—Risk & Ritualization

In phase II of the addiction cycle, risk and deception become the addict's tools to heighten gratification as he soothes his pain, choosing reward over his previous ethics and values.

As I dove deeper, I unveiled a steady deterioration of Kyle's sense of worthiness, further exacerbated by his inner shame. His desires and behavior fueled his guilt and magnified his initial pain caused by an unconfirmed earlier trauma. With intention to hide his new outlet, his success in deceiving others pleasured and empowered him to take risks to greater extremes.

As he became stressed and helpless to control addiction's temptations, defiance increased his euphoria. He planned midnight rituals to his computer as his family slept. He continually sheltered his inner conflicts with the comforts of porn, ultimately surrendering to his dependency and withdrawing any effort to seek help.

Phase III—Compulsive Sexual Behavior

The addict's preoccupation with online sex turns compulsive as his values become rewired by addiction's control.

Kyle schemed for other opportunities to engage in his addiction while avoiding the risk of discovery. At this stage, porn entered his workplace. His insatiable desires to experiment grew richer, and he lost the ability to resist as his obsession escalated, risking discoveries of illicit downloads through business fax lines.

As the cycles grew stronger and more chronic, Kyle became powerless to control his urges at home and at work. He rationalized his alone times and negative behaviors, disengaging from his marriage and becoming more controlling and resentful of its demands. His core values were replaced with cravings for a heightened euphoria, and he entered addiction's next stage of experimentation, rewarding his ego with hookers to engage in his newfound discoveries of sex acts.

Phase IV—Despair

At this stage, the addict rationalizes his defiance, risking everything important to him to sustain the relationship that soothes his pain. His obsession has escalated to a dependency with repercussions, and his shame is replaced by empowerment, eroding all sense of true reality.

Eventually, Kyle's addiction corrupted his mind as it demanded constant attention. It defined his schedule, finances, friendships, and activities centered around its power to reward. Still perceived by outsiders as a devoted husband and father, he successfully managed a new life of duality. Yet when he sat down at midnight to his computer, his pseudo-counterpart provided his weakness an antidote of authority, energizing and empowering him as he provided email subscribers with reviews of new hookers who could satisfy their unspeakable needs.

Then, with one indiscretion within the walls of his work cubicle, Kyle's world came crashing down as he lost his job, family, and reputation. His bank accounts were disclosed to a divorce court, and his indiscretions unveiled computer downloads of more than two thousand images of underage girls. He confronted a crossroads, where addiction recovery was his choice. However, he continued to justify himself as the victim, glaring unrepentantly at the law in his rearview mirror. His new sense of reality would soon cost him severely as he drove to Arizona to birth a new life and a more aggressive addiction.

A Time for Letting Go

Dear Kyle,

My life has become self-absorbed in the aftermath of despair. Each day, I tirelessly put one baby step forward with each obstacle: a broken foot, a house that won't sell, and now, remodelers. Although positive, the move to our new home was painful, forcing me to look past many memories as I look forward to a new future for me and the kids.

As I ready the house for sale, each item in our old house, from furnishings to a picture frame, holds a memory. I pass each room, pack a box, or work in the yard, and relive our past. Every time I visit, I replay our lives there during the past five years. Its superficial beauty is only a small portion of what I've lost. As this house now sits nearly vacant, awaiting a new family, I cannot fully let go. It holds captive the memories, remaining personal belongings, and my equity which will eventually enable me to finally move on upon its sale.

Amid my financial burdens, your lies continued to broadside me in divorce court with the unveiling of an unknown bank account. I was astonished, assuming this to be where you hid funds from your prostitution side hustle. I was numb, trying to appear strong as I disguised the pain of still-bleeding wounds. Our lives built on love and security have been shattered by your countless betrayals. I may never learn when or why they began and will *always wonder how long my loving, devoted husband was nothing more than a mere illusion.*

Deep inside, I know I deserve better, and that God loves me and will provide for me and the kids. I don't know when my pain will ever subside, but I trust He is walking this journey alongside me to the end. I also now see how He offered you multiple opportunities for change as He softened my heart for you repeatedly when I wanted to leave, despite my love.

Brick by brick, I'm trying to build a new life, with my first goal to gain new financial security. Expenses are mounting, and your child support income is now gone due to your second addiction-related job loss in Arizona.

So much is dependent on my strength. Failure is not an option. After nearly two years spent living in trauma, I'm desperate for a breakthrough. I hang on tightly, gripping onto my faith. Some days, I feel as if I am just dangling in the wind, but never without confidence. As when we lost our son, I know the day of healing will eventually come.

Kathy

Chapter 7

The Chaos of Reconstruction

Verse of Reflection

Come to me, all you who are weary and burdened, and I will give you rest. Take my yoke upon you and learn from me, for I am gentle and humble in heart, and you will find rest for your souls. For my yoke is easy and my burden is light.

—Matthew 11:28–30

The weeks rolled into months as I continued the process of self-discovery through support groups. I began to gain a new perspective regarding life as a single parent to two children. However, each day, legal waiting-games and fears for the future caused me distraction as I rebuilt my emotional strength.

As I prepared to move forward, every piece of furniture and knickknack required I sort through our past. The conclusion of the divorce settlement and deed transfer prohibited me from liquidating our home until our fall hearing. Kyle's forthcoming indictment also awaited the determination of charges pending the FBI's computer forensics team's final report. Once charged, he would be titled a fugitive on the run, subject to extradition and imprisonment as an accused sex offender.

My former traditional suburban life now resembled a cataclysmic crime novel. The rebuilding of my shattered world sat on hiatus as I watched and waited for the anticipated nightmare of Kyle's imprisonment, leaving me on the edge. I also remained aware of the threat posed by Child Protective Services. If the authorities confirmed I had any knowledge of Kyle's activities while living with our children, I could be charged as an unfit parent and lose custody of them altogether.

I yearned desperately for a new stability. Then, my fourteen-year-old daughter, Katie, served as God's messenger when she presented me with a surprise letter of her support:

> *Mom, I can't say I fully understand and appreciate everything you do and why. Even if I don't, I still want to thank you for faking a smile when I needed it most. I thank you for tearing out your hair to understand my math homework, and I'm thanking you for being courageous when it matters most. I'm thanking you for being "Mom."*

My child tossed me a lifeline during a difficult time with her confidence in my judgment despite her confusion. As I accepted her gift, I responded with a long hug and softly kissed her head. Through her gesture of unconditional love, God spoke to me, reminding me of His lesson when we don't understand our trials and heartaches. As Katie trusted me, we're called to do likewise and have faith in our heavenly Father, who knows our needs and loves us so much.

When she left the room, I realized our family had spent six months enduring trauma. We needed a vacation break somewhere, away from all the anxiety of the past several months. With limited funds, I had no idea where to go.

"Why don't you enjoy some time in Florida?" my mother asked.

"Mom, I can't go there. You remember why, don't you?"

"Why?" she responded.

"Because that was our last vacation with Ryan before he died. The memories are too painful. I swore I'd never return to that place."

"Let me go with you. Maybe you could instead find some comfort in those memories," Mom said.

And so, we flew to her condo in Cape Coral, Florida, with our new kitten, Boots, in her carrier beneath our seats.

Surprisingly, I found solace during our trip as we built the first of new memories without Kyle and Ryan. This place had represented family togetherness during my childhood, and I discovered an unexpected comfort in reminders of my son's presence as we escaped the turmoil controlling our lives. I also treasured time spent focusing on the kids as my mom focused on me, prior to her dramatic mental decline. During this trip, I shared with her the anguish of my newfound knowledge of Kyle's affair with a prostitute, which produced a child. Throughout my mother's remaining life until her death three years later, I would return her compassion and devotion to me as her demeanor and memory faded due to Alzheimer's.

Upon returning home, and after eight months of mental

turbulence, I functioned productively on some days while, on others, I lived life in the moment. As I prepared to list our home, continual and unexpected household repairs tested my patience and sapped my emotional strength during the months leading to our divorce. First, the garbage disposal, dishwasher, and clothes dryer malfunctioned, followed by the TV and CD player, the garden fountain, and the air conditioner. Lastly, my car went into the shop for repair. Overwhelmed and frustrated, I locked my keys and purse inside the rental car. Financial strains continued to mount, and it seemed nothing worked seamlessly anymore in my world. I felt my life was going nowhere.

Each week, my list of to-dos grew, with new tasks mounting before the old ones were completed. As a newly single working mom, I was consumed by the growing list of responsibilities, with each day spoken for far in advance. At the end of the day, I relaxed with my favorite cabernet, savoring the slight numbing effect on those many stressful days. Then one evening, as I chopped onions and peppers for our fajita dinner, I felt the pangs of withdrawal when I realized I was all out of wine. I seriously contemplated a special trip to the store to pick up a bottle. This was a turning point for me, forcing me to realize a potential problem on the horizon that could ultimately threaten the vision ahead. Retreating to alcohol would prevent me from giving them the childhood they deserved, and I was unwilling to exchange their future for another parent's stronghold.

As expenses multiplied, I accepted a full-time position in retail sales to create cash flow while searching for a higher-paying job during the start of an economic recession. With new work demands, the house quickly became a time and financial burden, requiring help I could not afford.

One day, I decided to focus on much-needed housework while enjoying the basic tasks of tending to my children. At that time, Katie had begun learning guitar. She played quietly in her room and toyed with writing songs. I smiled as I emptied her trash filled with crushed notebook paper of her discarded lyrics, secretly opening the pages to read her potential songs. I then unraveled as I read the words on the page with fear and astonishment.

"Oh God, she's cutting!" I gasped.

The thought of losing her, too, made me panic. I immediately ran downstairs and scheduled an appointment with her pediatrician that same day. In a whirlwind after school, I drove my daughter to her doctor for a head-to-toe check that revealed hidden razor lines on her inner thighs. She believed she could escape anxiety and pain by releasing blood through her secret wounds.

Had I not discovered her song lyrics that day, the chill of what could have occurred in time made me shudder. My emotions fell into the deep end, and the burden made me feel I had reached my breaking point. The thought of losing another child was too much to bear. My maternal instinct ignited my focus toward finding the right counselor to help my daughter reconcile her personal pain.

"Amy, can you help me?" I asked my DivorceCare co-facilitator after class.

"What do you need?" she asked.

"I need a counselor for my fourteen-year-old daughter. I discovered she's been cutting, and I'm unsure where to turn," I said anxiously.

"The church has several great counselors for kids in that age group. I'll get you a list of them to call and see who's covered by your insurance."

A few days passed. I received an email from Amy, and I began to call counselors and sift through the prescheduling process to begin Katie's healing and block sessions on my busy calendar. The phone then rang, identifying a call from Arizona.

"Hello?"

"Mrs. Lackey, my name is Eugene. I'm a friend of your husband," said the male on the other end of the line.

"What kind of friend?" I asked suspiciously.

"I'm calling to let you know he's been arrested."

"What happened?" I realized this time was bound to come. But who was this person in Kyle's life, and why was he calling me?

"Kyle was arrested for a traffic violation driving home last night from a bar. The police found out about his indictment from his license plate, and he's now in jail."

"What happens now?" I asked, "And why would he give you my number?"

"He asked me to move his truck and put his things in storage. But I don't have his keys. I wondered if you have one you could send me."

"No, I don't. Kyle and I are separated. Besides, why would he ask you?"

"He told me what was going on and asked me to help him if he got arrested. He wants me to get his truck out of the parking lot and drive it to his apartment. He also has bail money in the glove compartment."

"Where exactly is he living now?" I asked.

Eugene responded, giving me the name of the apartment community without hesitation.

I grabbed a pen and paper. "Listen, the leasing office will need to be notified because Kyle will next be extradited to Dallas, where he'll face charges. I'll need to call his cousin, who serves as his power of attorney, to take it from here."

After we hung up, I looked up the phone number for the apartment community in Tucson, where Kyle had been living.

"How can I help you today?" the leasing agent asked.

"This is Kathryn Lackey. I understand you have a tenant named Kyle Lackey. He is my husband but we are currently separated." I took a deep breath. "I was recently informed that he's been arrested. He won't be returning to his apartment, and I wondered how to get a key to collect his belongings." When the words left my mouth, it hit me that either his appointed power of attorney (his cousin) or I would need to travel to Arizona to assume that responsibility.

"You're not listed as an emergency contact, but he has listed his power of attorney. He's the only person who can receive a key." She continued, "Quite honestly, we have filed an eviction notice for unit #91, tenant Kyle Lackey, for disruptive conduct and complaints by his neighbors."

"What kind of conduct?" I asked.

"Mr. Lackey has been disruptive from the onset of his lease. The neighbors have complained of loud parties coming from his apartment. Some of our female tenants have also complained about his rude gestures and harassing comments to young girls at the pool, which we will not tolerate. He has also been inviting some of the younger, college-age female tenants to his apartment," she complained.

"I don't know what to say. I don't have an excuse for him and am so sorry. So, what happens now to his belongings if you evict him before a family member can get there to collect them? I live in Texas, and his power of attorney is in Minnesota," I said.

"We need someone to retrieve his items immediately. If someone cannot collect his things, then we will be forced to donate them and trash the items that are not donatable."

"All right, I'll get in touch with his emergency contact right now and ask him to make arrangements to clear out Kyle's apartment. And what happens to his parked vehicle?" I asked.

"We'll have it towed if it is not removed from the parking lot," she responded.

We hung up, and I immediately called Kyle's next-in-command with the news. "Yes, Kyle called me from the jail. I'm on my way out there to wipe up his debris again," he replied.

After I hung up, I realized Kyle's addiction was now in full force as it navigated his behaviors to a place of extreme danger. His previous engagements with hookers had escalated to attempted encounters with unsuspecting young girls. I was gravely concerned for their safety, lured by the excitement of his private parties but blind to his ulterior sexual motives. Assault or rape could be next. I was relieved he'd been captured to prevent the potential for additional crimes as his addiction amplified. I was also hit with the reality that he would soon be returning to Dallas.

That night, I attempted to relax from the day's phone calls after getting the kids to bed. I retired early but was awakened by noises outside at one o'clock in the morning. *Who could that be outside at this hour?*

My bedroom sat at the back of the house on the main level. I suddenly heard the back gate open, and flashlights beamed into the windows. There were the voices of multiple people roaming through my backyard. I feared turning on the lights or going to the door. *What's happening? Am I about to get robbed? Who is outside, and why are they surrounding the house?*

I put on my robe and snuck toward the front of the house to protect my children upstairs. Still asleep in their beds, I couldn't reach them due to the large stairway window enabling the perpetrators to see me. I was scared and didn't know what to do or how to keep my children safe.

Just then, I heard voices outside. They were in the front of the house, shining their flashlights through the front windows. I ran to the pantry to hide, trapped and isolated as they circled my home. After several minutes, I heard silence. *Did they leave?*

I slowly opened the pantry closet and heard nothing. Hugging the walls to avoid being seen, I carefully peeked around the edge of each downstairs window. I saw no one outside. We were safe again, but I was too afraid to call the police and did not want to awaken the children. Disturbed and frightened by what had just happened, I checked on them and went back to bed, realizing how vital it had become to move away from this house we had shared with a criminal to a home that offered a new beginning and more security.

Scared for our protection, I tried to stay awake and keep watch for the remainder of the night. However, I was exhausted from fear and drifted off to sleep until the alarm awakened me. Partially conscious, I rolled over to turn it off, realizing it was not the alarm ringing but the phone instead.

"Hello?" I answered, hoping this three a.m. call might explain the strange occurrence just hours earlier, but no one replied. Instead, there was dead space and the sound of someone breathing heavily into the phone. Again, I was caught off guard. There were background sounds, but I couldn't determine the call's location. This was clearly a crank call.

Annoyed, I began to hang up. But just then, the person on the other end finally spoke. "Kyle . . ." he whispered slowly and repeatedly as he cast fear with his slow deep breaths.

"Hello, who is this?" I asked forcefully. By this time, I had become very impatient.

The caller hung up. There was no caller ID. This was clearly someone's threat, and I would soon become his victim if I did not act upon his warning immediately.

Numb from fear, I was unable to rest for the remainder of the night, feeling I'd again met the devil on that phone call. The first time had been in Kyle's attorney's office. *Was this call related to the people who had surrounded my house?*

Relieved by the morning light after a night of terror, I rushed the kids off to school, ready to end my waiting game to move forward. It was time to call out for help and protection.

A Vacation to the Past

Dear Kyle,

Now, with you gone, I could finally slip away from the stress of job-hunting, divorce, and emotional withdrawals as I tried to accept the reality of losing you. A vacation was not in the budget, but a week in Florida at my family's condo afforded me much-needed time to think and regroup while I sorted through all that has happened.

Ten years ago, I swore I'd never return to this place where we'd vacationed just months before Ryan's death. I just knew the memories of my last joys with him would be more than I could bear. Instead, I found a strange comfort as I recalled the two of us throwing his fishing pole into the canal and collecting broken shells along the coast of Sanibel Island. After only a short time, I revisited precious memories I'd never been fully able to capture. I also realized that the sadness of him now gone did not exceed the agony of my new loss, as losing you both is heartbreaking. I felt battered and broken, and my soul numb, as I faced an unknown future without you also.

With more ease than expected, as I toured the grounds of that last trip, I recalled treasured memories, finding pureness in those memories previously blinded by my own pain. Our times together were spent with love and a mother's devotion to her child. Despite other demands with a new baby, I set aside time with my eldest child when we could bond as mother and son. I found comfort in revisiting those memories we created a decade ago.

As I process life without you, memories of our times together on our family vacations are not as pure and comforting as those with Ryan. While relieving my many questions about your strange behaviors, my newfound knowledge now surfaces new questions that remain unanswered:

- *How many family trips did you escape briefly to satisfy your hunger for hookers?*
- *When did you become a mere illusion of the perfect family man?*
- *And when was your love and devotion to us nothing more than a lie?*

But the most troubling is, how could you know of my loneliness for so long and intimately and yet pursue such unfaithfulness without conscience or remorse? How many vacations, in addition to half a lifetime together, was I deceived as I chose to build a future with you?

As the kids watched TV, I poured my heart out to Mom, an Alzheimer's patient who couldn't fully comprehend your betrayals behind my pain. Regardless, I leaned on her emotional support as she held my hand. She then cried with me as I shared my discovery of the child born to your favorite hooker the spring following your summer affair. Before you met me for marriage counseling just a few blocks away, you visited your pregnant mistress. Accepting your love for her is a torment that is truly too much to bear.

The wonderful times we previously spent as a family are now tainted with the impurity of your betrayals. How can I revisit the picture albums of each trip without wonder and regret as I imagine your hidden activities behind the scenes?

Despite my initial prediction, I am glad I escaped to this place where I found unexpected comfort when I lacked the ability to find any healing at all. It signifies family, including my childhood years and memories with my children apart from you. These times together were pure and unspoiled, and so will be the memories we create for the future. My maternal bond with them will survive the bitterness of your past.

Kathy

Chapter 8

The Indictment

Verse of Reflection

God is our refuge and strength,
an ever-present help in trouble.
Therefore we will not fear, though the earth give way
and the mountains fall into the heart of the sea,
though its waters roar and foam
and the mountains quake with their surging.

—Psalm 46:1–3

I picked up the phone to call the only person I knew who could provide immediate protection. I dialed the county clerk's office.

"Can I please speak with Amy Smith?"

"Hi, Kathy, how are you? This is a surprise," Amy answered.

"I need your help again if you don't mind. I'm sorry for calling you at work, but I remembered you worked at the county clerk's office. I wondered if you might have a recommendation for a good attorney. My attorney has not made much progress, and I need a restraining order quickly. Kyle has been indicted, and I just experienced the scariest night of my life."

"I can recommend a few, but Wardon Spencer (affectionately called Spence) is one of the best. Would you like me to give you his number?"

"Yes, please," I answered. "That would be great."

I immediately called the number. Mr. Spencer's assistant transferred me to his office.

"Hello, Mr. Spencer?"

"Yes. My friends call me Spence. My assistant said you have an urgent matter."

"I appreciate you taking my call. Amy Smith from the county clerk's office recommended I give you a call. She's an acquaintance of mine through DivorceCare. She thought you may be able to help me. I've filed for divorce and do not have confidence in my current attorney. My husband has been indicted and will be extradited back to Texas any time now. I'm afraid for my family's safety with people surrounding my house and strange calls in the middle of the night. I need help."

"That was probably the police looking for him now that he's been indicted. Can you come into the office now?" he asked.

"I'll be there shortly." I disregarded my disheveled morning appearance and threw on my cap as I headed for my car.

I drove into downtown McKinney and found his office in an old Victorian house off the old McKinney main square. The door squeaked as it opened, and I could smell the age of history among the entryway's high ceilings and antiques.

I was guided to the parlor, where the lawyer would soon meet me. As he entered, I looked up from my chair, greeting him with fear and trepidation displayed on my face.

"Thank you for meeting me so soon," I said as I shook his hand.

"Of course. This is an important matter," he responded in a reserved tone. "Now sit down and tell me everything from start to finish."

I sat down in a chair by the window and began to tell him my story, fighting the tears streaming down my face as I looked down at the floor. "I'm sorry, I just can't look at anyone as I tell you all that's happened. It's too horrifying."

"That's okay. Whatever makes you feel comfortable," he replied.

After I finished, he gave a deep sigh of compassion, then stoically outlined the next steps for my protection.

"Follow me to my office," Spence said, while next escorting me up the beautiful Victorian bannister stairway to sign papers and collect a retainer.

After I left his office, my new attorney then petitioned the court for a prompt divorce hearing and an emergency restraining order. Before the day's end, he called to inform me of his urgent meeting with the new judge amid her preparations to leave town, and her prompt signature on a restraining order. Spence's actions were perfectly timed.

He further informed me it was fortunate this judge had been assigned to my case. She'd been left to raise four children alone in her own divorce following her husband's affairs. It had been a highly publicized scandal. This judge proved to be God's protection from the man I'd once trusted with my life.

In the weeks leading up to our divorce trial, I was filled with dreaded anticipation of Kyle's extradition to Dallas, the timing for his return, and his resumed contacts if he posted bail. I alerted neighbors and friends, asking them to please keep watch on the house and my children when I worked late hours. My anxiety grew at the thought of seeing him again and the chaos to follow as I sat waiting for justice to run its course.

The emotional load became too great, and I finally confided in my pastor.

"Be cautious. You may have once had feelings for him, but this man is evil! He is not your friend," he firmly counseled.

The longer I lived with unknowns, the more I began to accept the reality of the monster this man had become. I recalled my recent conversation with the leasing agent in Arizona, and cringed at Kyle's potential to cause trouble in his addiction's next stage. At this point, he had self-destructed, losing all his former credibility and dignity as he surrendered to addiction's control.

I feared not only becoming his victim in court but also becoming his target. Now able to piece together his mindset and anticipate his actions, I was knowledgeable of the avoidance and bitterness behind his addictive behaviors. His intention was to plot vengeance and justify his actions against his opposition, which currently was me. Ultimately, my financial dependence would become his last tool to steer negotiations toward his favor. As my faith was tested, he would underestimate its strength, pridefully confident that I was more dependent on him than on God's safety and provisions. He was wrong.

One evening, upon returning home from after-school sports, the kids went upstairs to prepare for bed, and I could finally relax after a long day. I sat in Kyle's chair and turned on the TV. As I kicked off my shoes, I abruptly sat up, shocked by his mugshot on the late evening news. *He's back!*

Alarmed, I sat back and took a deep breath, knowing I was now prepared with a protective order that would enforce his distance if he returned to disrupt our lives again.

As he awaited trial following his bail, Kyle began calling me. Initially, we spoke civilly, and he provided a forwarding address for his mail. Then, he began to call more frequently with manipulative cries for pity. I had done all I could do to help him, and far more than he deserved. He needed to help himself. My focus now was to plan a new life for me and our children as our divorce neared conclusion.

One warm October day, we finally met at the Collin County Courthouse. As we huddled individually with our attorneys in preparation, our twenty-year marriage would become open to legal scrutiny as our belongings were divided between us as mere commodities.

The attorneys pleaded their case arguments to the judge. In response, the judge turned to my husband. "Mr. Lackey, please stand." She continued, "Ownership of the home and financial accounts you previously shared with your wife will now be passed to Kathryn Lackey, including all financial obligations and deeds. You will maintain ownership only of your personal belongings, your individual bank account at Compass Bank, and the truck vehicle titled to you. Your wife will receive all remaining proceeds within your employment brokerage 401K account, except for $30,000 for your personal use."

"As for the children, Kathryn Lackey is granted sole guardianship. Your visitation is permitted only upon their request, as you no longer represent a positive paternal role model. In consideration of your indictment charges, you are granted supervised visitation only at a court-appointed facility. You will continue to provide support for your children, including their health insurance through your military retirement."

As Kyle's lawyer disputed the final ruling, the attorneys approached the bench. The three whispered together. Shortly afterward, the judge concluded our hearing with the strike of her gavel.

I looked over at my former husband, astonished by the

generous gift by the judge's final ruling. Kyle, in turn, stood stripped of his pride and his fatherhood. He'd now lost all rights to his achievements, including his children. As he left the courtroom, his eyes met mine with contempt, unremorseful for his harms to our family.

My attorney approached and congratulated me on the ruling.

"Spence, we didn't ask for that settlement. You said we would each receive a 50/50 split of our belongings. What happened?"

"The judge said you would need every penny. She saw the indictment, and knew he will most likely see prison," he responded. "She sympathized, knowing what lies ahead for you as he faces a jury."

"And the Compass Bank account? We don't have an account at that bank."

"You both don't, but he does," he said.

As I headed home, I stopped by Compass Bank to inquire about this balance. While confidentiality prevented information other than an active account, I perceived this to be the private bank account where Kyle financed his addiction for hookers using an initial deposit of his company's relocation dollars.

From the desk of Kathryn Lackey . . .

Wounds of Reflection

❦

Dear Kyle,

I have just taken a sleeping pill and am now waiting for its effects. I've not slept in two nights, and I'm desperate to rest from the drain of emotional stress.

Last night, I fought the temptation to call you, hoping to share even a mere morsel of the agony you've inflicted on me. Each job interview lacks a reward for an accomplishment toward a new career but instead is a preparation for a survival transition caused by your addiction illness.

I cannot relax with reminders of your infidelities and crimes all around me, such as last night when I watched a TV show that depicted a murderer of his sexual conquests, all who ultimately became his victims. Yes, it was fiction, a mere episode for entertainment. However, mine is reality. Although in a different manner, you still sacrificed women to your shame.

The reality of what you have done has grown more intense as you now face indictment. I want redemption for my suffering, but you are incapable of any remorse, consumed by your own panic. Your selfishness has defined our past three years in Dallas, our present, and has shattered our future. Everything I hoped, dreamed, and believed to be secure is gone forever. The ground beneath me has caved, and I am engulfed in the dirt and debris of your lies and their domino of consequences.

Tell me, was anything about our marriage true? Without my knowledge, I've been living a lie, an illusion of comfort, love, and security. Now you are jobless, a divorce is pending, and the house will be sold. Our children's former security will no longer exist. Is this what you meant all those times you proclaimed to me, "I love you"?

I will lose our home and our family's togetherness. I now ache from the many memories I once believed were built on love, happiness, and our commitment to each other and our kids. I didn't realize, as I do now, that commitment was mine alone. I am now one, not two. My pain drives me to support groups to regurgitate emotions and write letters to you, hoping to capture some resemblance of your presence. In your twisted mind, do you in any way release your pain of losing me or only the lifestyle that you gave up? You may grieve what you had. I grieve what I thought I had.

As much as I loved you, I stayed with you in my obedience to God's will. He was on your side even when I wavered as I mapped my departure. He gave me a heart of forgiveness when I wanted to leave, and I suffered long and hard in prayer. I finally made the decision to recommit to our marriage, believing you had also. But in the end, I was betrayed by my most trusted confidant, my lifelong partner, and I often feel also by God, aware of your indiscretions as I suffered in silence. Your definition of love has hurt me more than words can describe. I pray that one day, I will heal from this pain, too.

I'm truly glad for the efforts you previously made toward employment to support your family. Now, as you return to Dallas to face judgment, I know you live each day on the edge. I want to support and encourage you, hoping you'll recognize the past and attempt addiction recovery. But my pain is too great. I can't stop the wounds from bleeding. I'm open flesh. I was your prey. Lots of time will be required to heal these wounds.

Kathy

Chapter 9

The Judgments

Verse of Reflection

Do not fear, for I have redeemed you;
I have summoned you by name; you are mine.
When you pass through the waters,
I will be with you;
and when you pass through the rivers,
they will not sweep over you.
When you walk through the fire,
you will not be burned;
the flames will not set you ablaze.
For I am the LORD your God,
the Holy One of Israel, your Savior.

—Isaiah 43:1b–3a

In the weeks following the final divorce hearing, my faith became the architect of our future, and my children, the mortar that glued me together. I began to construct a new life for our threesome, day by day, brick by brick, starting with the sale of our house. With full ownership of the deed, this sale would finally relieve financial stress and home maintenance demands while providing a fresh start in a more secure home unknown to my ex-husband and his crime partners. I navigated the challenges of our family's reconstruction, still cautioned by one more legal round to follow. Round one concluded our divorce. Round two would define Kyle's indictment charges, potentially subjecting him to a twenty-year prison sentence.

Each day, I got up and went to work as our primary provider, much like my ex-husband had done for many years. I accepted my new role as the sole breadwinner with extreme motivation. I placed enormous burdens on myself to do everything right, shielding the kids from drama with the distractions of our daily routines. Mentally drained, I longed for happiness once again, and often, just a simple hug to recharge my batteries.

With the divorce behind, I was now legally a single mom open to dating opportunities. In my prime at the age of 44, I looked my best, dropping thirty pounds effortlessly due to stress. Interested men at work approached me, and friends invited me back into the social scene as they encouraged me to "get out and meet people." But I had no interest for a new intimacy or closeness as I suffered the psychological aftermath of my ex-husband's repeated sexual betrayals.

Yes, I longed for the unconditional shelter of a strong man's arms to renew my strength. I yearned to feel desirable and attractive again, but instead, I felt defiled by the looks of men, genderless, a mere shell, unable to internalize attraction or any sexual desire at all. Kyle's lies and infidelities had stripped me of my femininity. I now perceived desire as unpleasant and dirty. I lost my sense of purpose and value, trapped in the belittlement of his shame. I was dangerously fragile, overwhelmed by the complexity of my present and future. At this stage, I decided not to date and chose to stay focused and alone, realizing I was hollow and had nothing left to give after my trauma.

The weeks following our divorce were pleasantly uneventful and silent. Our family's significant fall holidays went by, each more painful than its predecessor as I accepted our marriage's end and Kyle's consequences. First Halloween, his birthday, and then Thanksgiving went by. Previously, those were family days filled with fun and togetherness. Now, they were just gloomy reminders of past happiness selfishly snatched away by the hands of an addict.

The Indictment

The November day of Kyle's indictment hearing finally arrived. Ironically, his court appearance occurred on the twenty-first anniversary of our wedding. Surprisingly, the district attorney extended a rare second offer for a ten-year probation with a $10,000 fine. In exchange, Kyle would carry a card providing his public record as a registered sex offender. At a legal crossroads, he pled guilty and accepted the plea bargain he'd refused once before. He would otherwise face a twenty-year sentence if the case progressed to trial.

Thank you, God. I see you in the shadows, I thought as He made one last provision for Kyle's redemption.

But Kyle had other plans.

He went on with his life to seek employment wherever he could. Now a free man with conditions and boundaries, he could no longer visit a public location that would expose him to children within five hundred feet, and he would wear an ankle bracelet while serving his ten-year probation, a precursor to a potential violation.

His contact finally subsided with the restraining order. We sold the house nine months later, during a recession, and relocated close by to a home in the kids' same school district, among their friends. While my choices to move anywhere in the country included my childhood home in New York to care for Mom, I focused on minimizing my children's transition as they also healed, now without a father. I concealed our new address from Kyle for our safety, and the children requested no visitation, fearing the man who had caused us such pain. I never insisted on visitation, nor did I restrain their requests to see him. I remained neutral and respected their emotions. All I could do was compassionately offer them the love and security of a devoted parent and a safe home in a neighborhood that they trusted.

Three months following our move, the kids left for school on a beautiful, crisp October day. I snuck back into bed to indulge in a few more hours of sleep on my day off from work. I changed the alarm from six to nine in the morning. Added sleep was a privilege, but there was no sense wasting an entire morning.

At 8:57 a.m., the phone rang.

"Hello?" I answered.

"Mrs. Lackey? This is Officer Sheridan from the Collin County Sheriff's Department. Does Kyle Lackey, by any chance, live there with you?"

"No, we are divorced. I now have a protective order that prevents him from coming within five hundred feet of me or the kids. He also cannot contact me in any way, shape, or form," I responded. Then reality struck, and it dawned on me that Kyle was in some sort of trouble once again.

I pried further. "Why do you ask? Is he in trouble? Has something happened?"

"Well, yes, ma'am. His probation has been revoked. We are trying to locate him to bring him in."

My heart sank. Would his series of bad decisions ever end? Did he not realize how fortunate he was to be gifted another chance of parole when, for all reason, he did not deserve it?

"Why? What happened?" I asked.

"He was found in possession of child pornography."

Again? How could he be so stupid?

"Do you know where he is staying?" the officer asked.

There was nothing I could do to protect him now. I refused to lower myself to a criminal charge by warning and enabling a felon.

"The last time we spoke, he was staying at an extended-stay motel in Richardson. Let me see if I can find the address," I replied as I rummaged through my huge divorce folder.

The officer uttered the address before I could find it. It was the address on record with his probation officer.

"Yes, that's it," I confirmed.

Before hanging up, the officer thanked me.

"If you don't mind, how did you know he was in possession of child pornography?"

"Well, ma'am, we have internet search records from his phone that violate his probation. He has also failed to report to his probation appointments."

That was it. A double offense. That's why he was in trouble!

"Will you let me know when you find him? This is not the man I was married to. We were together for over twenty years, and he was a wonderful man before this addiction took over. I still care what happens to him."

"Yes, we'll let you know when we find him. Thank you. Goodbye."

I could tell from the officer's voice that he was surprised I cared at all anymore. Frankly, I wondered myself.

I lay back down on my bed and clung to my pillow. Kyle's decisions ceased my ability to understand him as I once had. Strangely, it felt like just yesterday when our mere thoughts were congruent before we spoke. I was sad and so very disappointed, but strangely, no longer fearful. I realized this man, controlled by his sexual addiction, had succumbed to its final destruction, and he would return to prison, a consequence of his own doing. There was no helping him now, and no further opportunity for remorse.

Absent of panic for the first time, I got up and made coffee, let the dog out, checked my emails and my bank account, and proceeded to go over my to-do list for the day over breakfast.

Hmmm. Waffles would be nice today. It's my day off, and I don't want cereal.

I enjoyed my waffles, then prioritized my day before the kids got home from school. I did not call anyone to share the news, cry, or encourage sadness. Instead, I savored the sweetness of my buttered waffles and syrup. After breakfast, I walked the dog and prayed as I again took God's hand in trust.

I recognized a new confidence in my response to Kyle's final violation and had faith that our lives would gain further strength in time. This day began the first of many where I would ask God to show me how something good could come from something so bad as I surrendered Kyle one last time to His plan.

The Conviction

The day prior to his trial, I went to see Kyle in the Collin County Detention Facility. While I needed his signature on military documents for the kids' insurance, I also needed to see him one last time to find closure while I still could.

I sat anxiously in the large entry area as I waited for my name to be called. I had no idea what to expect from this experience or Kyle's demeanor, now divorced and soon to become a convict. I waited for close to an hour. Finally, they called my name as part of a group escorted to a meeting room where I would meet Kyle behind glass.

Our meeting was brief, avoiding argumentation. He was curt and distant when he spoke. I updated him on the kids' happenings, and he asked me to take good care of them in his absence.

I recall my emptiness as I was forced to accept the man now clothed in an orange jumpsuit, a new symbol of his crimes. His eyes were cold and calculating. He was no longer someone I knew. I left melancholy with deep regrets, as if it were his funeral, and swore I would never subject myself to seeing him in prison again. I wondered what the future held, if he would make it in prison or kill himself to escape a living hell. Time would tell.

Due to work obligations, the trial ensued without me. The day of his sentencing came in the days to follow.

On that sunny fall day in McKinney, Texas, I sat among strangers in the courtroom at the Collin County Courthouse to witness my ex-husband's fate. My children remained ignorant of my pain during their day at school as I shielded them from the confusion and drama of their father's shame. I entered the courtroom stoically and alone with no support, choosing a seat among bystanders where I felt comfortably transparent and unaffiliated with the accused.

I then saw the man I once called my husband enter the room, and my strength began to fade. I leaned over to an elderly gentleman seated on my right and softly asked if he would kindly hold my hand. Although I never met this man before, I desperately needed a hand to grip as I awaited the judge's verdict. I clutched it tightly, watching the body language of my ex-husband as he approached the bench. In his orange jumpsuit with shackles and chains clanging together around his ankles and wrists, he walked toward the judgment seat to receive the sentence that would transform our lives forever.

I then witnessed my college sweetheart and husband of two decades sentenced to a twenty-year prison term. His attorney had previously negotiated a ten-year probation and $10,000 fine with the district attorney, given no previous criminal record. This plea bargain served as Kyle's "get out of jail free" card. It was rare to receive the gift of no prison time amid his crimes, not once but twice. However, my husband repeatedly dared his pardons, denying any wrongdoing, resulting in a guilty verdict for possession and solicitation of child pornography.

"I never touched anyone!" Kyle responded adamantly in his defense. He never admitted guilt but manifested a fantasy of perceived innocence, declaring himself the real victim. His addiction rationalized his choices, birthed his double life, and destroyed our dreams. As a result, Kyle would next be escorted to Huntsville, Texas, a prison with a reputation as the most hellacious and dangerous in the state.

In disbelief, I was unable to cry. The moment was surreal as I questioned whether this was a dream or a reality of the devastation I had just witnessed. I was paralyzed by shock and felt no control of my present, just fog. His life was over. Drained of all emotion, I departed the courtroom and headed for my car, trying to accept that our lives had officially changed forever.

I repeated a question I'd asked many times before: How had this happened under my watch? Where was I, and could I have prevented this in any way? I remained shocked by his addiction's transgressions.

As I drove home, not knowing what to do next, God took my hand and led me moment by moment, day by day. He was in control, and I was finally free.

From the desk of Kathryn Lackey . . .

Crying in the Darkness

Dear Kyle,

Last night for me was terrible! It is so hard to resist calling you, but then what? I would talk, you'd then tune me out, accuse me of fighting, and the cycle would start again. Communicating with you is a vicious cycle. So, instead, I am writing you this letter to express my thoughts peacefully. I know I must stay away to move forward, but sometimes, this task is agonizing.

Where you are addicted to porn and sex with strangers, I am addicted to you and our family. The three of you are my life. As I mourned over Ryan, I now mourn over you as if you, too, have died. In a sense, you have. Your soul has died. The man I once loved surrendered to the pain within him that he could not confront or share with others. This is the same man I committed to. I again recommitted when divorce seemed the only option as our marriage deteriorated. Your love and devotion to your family should have stopped your choices, but the opposite is true. You are now gone, sacrificing your family in the shadow of your shame.

Each night I awaken, unable to sleep due to my heartache. Fortunately, I've learned to block visions of you with other women. But I still find myself unconsciously reaching for you, longing to hear your breath in my ear as we spoon. I want to put my arms around you and lay on your chest, but you're no longer there. I cry in the darkness for our lives as they once were, but this is the new reality I'm forced to accept.

The Kyle I knew is gone. I want to love and support you, but I am afraid of the person who now claims you and has cost all our lives. I want to believe my Kyle is still inside you, but that's no longer safe. You have jeopardized our family's safety, security, and our twenty-year marriage to a life of depravity. We will never be the same again. I unconsciously enabled you, absolving your lies in my ignorance. And now, I've come to believe God finally needed to reveal the truth for my protection. It was your very last chance for redemption from a life of duality.

I am astonished by our ending. Where I once stood defeated by our marriage as it spiraled, I am now hollow as I face my future without you. Your death would have been more straightforward. My inner security has plummeted into a bottomless pit. The memories I once treasured as signs of your love leave me bewildered and confused. How do I now find true meaning?

I recall you covering me on the sofa when I fell asleep, candles and wine with dinner when I returned home, and your attentiveness when I became sick. I believed you loved me but now accept these sweet memories as mere lies fabricated by a narcissist. The man I once thought to be true now possesses a dark side, and my newly discerned trust is only for the unexpected. You have disappeared, but my love has not, and thus my heart continues to throb night after night.

I don't know when or if you will eventually read this letter, perhaps from a jail cell. But today, I stain these pages with the tears shed for the life we once shared. My children now depend on my strength and judgment. Yours is gone. You are gone. Our lives are gone forever.

Kathy

Chapter 10

Forgiveness

Verse of Reflection

Jesus said, "Father, forgive them, for they do not know what they are doing."

—Luke 23:34

$\mathcal{A}$s I watched my former husband disappear into a life of incarceration, I could have easily adopted bitterness and animosity upon conclusion to years of drama. His choices negatively impacted the lives of his family, placing us in sudden and severe hardships. An extradition, parole, and years later, his final prison release also produced ambivalence and fears for our security, fueling deep anger and lasting resentments for his many betrayals and selfish actions.

However, as I focused on healing and unveiling the nucleus of Kathy, I came to learn that the scars of unforgiveness held me in bondage. I felt shameful and ignorant as a victim of the sex addict's abuses, and I created self-limiting beliefs as strongholds that prevented my success in moving forward toward change.

Instead, I stood belittled and stripped of my self-worth, unable to envision the possibilities for personal accomplishments through my own God-given strengths. Broken and battered, I cloaked myself in a shawl of defeat and wore my role as a mere survivor. And that's where my story ended. In turn, I deprived myself of life's abundance, self-sabotaging relationships and career with unresolved insecurities and doubts surrounding my abilities as I accepted and wallowed in his shame.

I sometimes felt like I was paddling in the ocean's depths, with waves of struggle escalating my bitter memories and preventing closure to my pain. Kyle's shame incapacitated me from completely disengaging my identity as a byproduct of his crimes. I repeatedly belittled myself—*How could I not know?*—in turn, creating inner conflicts of anger that strangled my self-worth as I revisited my painful past. Worst of all, unforgiveness blinded me to see God's provisions as He then, and always, carried me through the deep quicksand to a solid ground of security while discovering healing and a new confidence in myself.

I learned valuable lessons during this journey and have now come to accept that the baggage of the past ultimately barricaded me from God's blessings for my future. I effectively vanquished my ability to receive them for many years despite my many cries in prayer. This was a travesty, for God wanted me not just to survive but to succeed through my individual gifts apart from my partner's shame.

God was the artist of my creation, and His ultimate desire was to write my story and introduce me to the child He created me to be. In turn, He would use my testimony of strength to share hope with other spouses and victims of sexual addiction, if I chose. But in my role purely as a survivor, I halted His purposeful plan to discover true healing and personal success. I also extinguished my ability to encourage others through my journey and help them along their personal walks toward partner addiction recovery.

Sadly, the journey to forgiveness required a lot of emotional work and self-reflection. This was a painful experience as I said goodbye to a man I trusted and believed completed me. Through research and counseling, I recognized codependency's negative contributions to addiction's cycles and also its unconscious attraction to new relationships. In turn, this enabled me to establish firm boundaries for current and future relationships as I healed and discovered new value in myself.

As I surpassed survivorship and discovered my true value, I unexpectedly unveiled a compassion for Kyle, entrapped by the mental illness of his addiction. I could finally separate myself from the downward spiral of his disease, which released me to ultimately find forgiveness for the true victim of addiction, my husband.

I concluded that I am validated individually as a child of God and valued as His alone. As I began to shed my role as addiction's victim, I was no longer subject to the emotional destruction of an exterior source. God's light in me was and is the only identity I need.

From the desk of Kathryn Lackey . . .

In the Wake of Parole

Dear Kyle,

I can't begin to tell you how many times I have attempted to write to you since your conviction. Although I wanted to share special moments with you about the kids, the scars of the past prevented me from prioritizing letters to you versus all the many other things I have to do as a single mom. But now, not knowing where you'll end up as you move through the court system, I am prioritizing communications so that you know I wish you the best.

Since I first learned of your "activities" in 2005, my life has been a whirlwind. First the divorce, then your indictment, all while relocating to another house. It was a very large load, and I had very little support. Shortly after we moved, I lost my job. Soon afterward, I was employed again and moving forward, just in time for my mother to fall and break her back in three places due to her osteoporosis. Unable to fly to her bedside and with no one else to assist, the financial drain of alternative full-time in-home care necessitated the pre-liquidation of her estate to pay for her care. Her Alzheimer's progressed rapidly toward the end. Her medical and in-home care became a huge burden to manage alone, and the stress of long-distance elder care put my personal health at risk with its many demands. In the fall of 2009, I moved Mom to assisted living. She was miserable. Six weeks following her move, she suffered a massive stroke, leaving her unconscious until her death three weeks later. It was horrible, and I have many regrets. I am still trying to close the remainder of her estate two years later.

Family and friends have chosen to remain largely absent during the past five years. I'm not quite sure why, and I know the kids have missed having an extended family network. Despite my turmoil with the divorce followed by Mom's health burdens, they have been amazing pillars of strength to me. I am enclosing a picture taken of all of us at Mom's eighty-eighth surprise birthday party, a few months before her death. Sadly, she did not recognize anyone but had a good time nonetheless. There is no doubt that she put much additional weight on me during an already difficult time. But I am grateful for her love for me and her grandchildren, and all her support as I adjusted to single parenthood.

Now for your children. Our daughter, Katie, is finishing her first year of college at Texas Woman's University. She graduated high school in the top 11 percent of her class, started college with twelve hours of dual college credits, and is attempting to enter the medical field as a biology major. Her ultimate hope is to become an equine chiropractor, which requires seven years of college credit. With her love of animals, I tried to lead her into vet medicine, but she could not deal with the sorrow of death, remembering the loss of our beloved dogs.

She has made great strides academically. Recently, she was offered a scholarship to the University of Findlay in Ohio, a top college for equestrian studies and vet care. We visited the campus over spring break, and I have full confidence that she will flourish there. It is perfect as a small Midwestern town, just large enough for entertainment and shopping. It fits her personality. She will double major in anatomy and equine studies.

The university has about three thousand students, all classes taught by full professors, and a small teacher/student ratio. They also offer a dedicated equine facility with three hundred horses. Katie will be given a horse of her own for six months to train and maintain as a part of her course curriculum. She will be in her glory! She also hopes to try out for the equestrian team, which I have not encouraged for her first year. You should be very, very proud of your daughter. She is truly amazing, and I will miss her dearly. She is a huge help and support, and we have a great and open relationship. At least I know she'll return to Dallas eventually and continue school at Parker University as she studies to become an animal chiropractor.

Grayson is fifteen, and now towers over me at six feet tall. He is a bean pole, much like you were growing up. This child tested gifted a few years ago in science and math. However, since losing his father, his grades have not illustrated his full potential. He is bored with academics and has shown little interest in sports up until recently. As a high school freshman, he tried out for the baseball team. Tryouts were extremely competitive, and unfortunately, he didn't make the team. This summer, I am signing him up for a four-week baseball camp to keep him interested and active in the sport. He will also attend driver's education and get his wisdom teeth removed. His grades are slowly improving. His main interest at school is German, and he hopes to travel to Germany after graduation. Between these events and getting Katie ready to relocate to out-of-state college, we have a busy summer ahead.

Both kids, like me, have a lot of scars from the damage caused to our family. Friends and family have distanced themselves, not knowing how to help or what to say. That has been difficult on us, especially during special events and holidays.

Your letters to Grayson have not been well received, as you should expect. He is an impressionable teenage boy largely in need of a male role model, and you are no longer here to fill that position. News of your future paroles raises worry in both their minds surrounding the surprises that could follow upon your release. Unable to absorb any more turmoil in our lives, I have asked your cousin and power-of-attorney to inquire how to have your paroles relocated away from our family. You will have to understand the parole board's decision to honor my request in restricting you from Collin County and from contacting us.

Kyle, I have no vengeance against you. I can only imagine the internal torture you must have experienced, living the double life you chose for yourself. Although it was painful, I am glad the truth finally came out so that you could get the help that you needed. It also relinquished me from your grip of manipulation. We have moved forward but are forever scarred. I have never degraded myself to negative references about you but rather have always told your children that you were sick. I offered multiple times to take them to see you in Bonham, Texas, during your time there in prison, but they refused to go.

Although you can potentially rebuild relationships with each of them eventually in the future, I believe it is best that you concentrate on yourself for right now and hold on to that hope for a later date. Katie is on a roll and concentrating on her future. She does not need to be pushed off course by emotions. Grayson, on the other hand, is too immature and impressionable at this age to absorb the extent of your problems and determine your level of honesty. There have been too many lies leading up to our family's destruction. Although you are welcome to continue with the occasional letter, I am requesting that you understand my request that you continue to let us all heal and rebuild for now. In the future, when Grayson is more grounded and emotionally mature, you can attempt to restore what you have since lost. For now, I ask that you concentrate on restoring yourself and building character and confidence, some of the characteristics that attracted me to you so many moons ago.

Good luck, Kyle. I am glad for you that you have a future parole opportunity, and I'll pray that you grab hold and treasure it, unlike you did before. You are capable of so much. Please relish this as God's gift and use it wisely.

Chapter 11

'Til Death Do Us Part

Verse of Reflection

Because of the tender mercy of [my] God,
    by which the rising sun will come to us from heaven
to shine on those living in darkness
    and in the shadow of death,
to guide our feet into the path of peace.

—Luke 1:78–79

*M*y husband's poor choices were repeated even following his release from prison. The continual threat to each of us revisited me with regret of the person he became amid his idol, the addiction. My guard relaxed while he served his prison sentence, but upon his release in March 2020, fear and PTSD returned with a vengeance.

As I slept each night praying for guidance as to what to do next, my protectors were a large candlestick and a butcher knife beneath my mattress. I tried to build a sense of control through the purchase of a home security system and shooting lessons as I planned my relocation to another state. Despite thirteen years of building a new life following his conviction, I feared the unforeseens of his next move. I realized I again had become a victim, uncertain of my future and safety once he was released from prison.

Frozen by the past, I recalled the details of the addiction and its destruction to our lives of happiness and stability. I recalled how my self-confidence continued to erode as I watched my ex-husband fade into another world of deception and crime. I then felt abandoned without him by my side to complete the future we'd planned for our lives and children. It remained inconceivable to me that his love for his family didn't intercept his decision for a life of duality. Instead, he surrendered to sin's grip, robbing his soul and the man we once loved.

My husband's addiction precluded his ability to find his way back to life, his family, and the blessings God had planned for him in this life. I did not have the power to change him, just as I hadn't the ability to cure him. He had a mental disease, and diseases require specialized help. Recovery is achieved through purposeful action. To recover, Kyle needed to seek change provided by the opportunities and resources extended to him, and envision the rewards of sobriety for himself and his family's future.

Now, at his funeral, I longed to find closure at last upon

his death. But instead, I unexpectedly revisited the role I previously inherited as a mere survivor of his transgressions. And that is truly how I felt as I sat under the cemetery tent that day, fixated on the white box housing the cremains of my ex-husband. The actions that led to that place in time were never forgotten or even pardoned by anyone who attended Kyle's funeral, especially his immediate family. I again felt left behind to suffer the consequences of his poor choices and decisions, much like a destructive cancer that goes into remission but later returns.

As I walked away at the end of the funeral, I resolved to shed the weight of the past, which had continually challenged my growth and success to move forward, knowing God promises never to waste a tear. I trusted Him to eventually unfold His purpose for our pain, and prayed with hope and anticipation: God, please show me how good can birth from something so bad.

Since that time, I have learned to ask for God's transformation consistently and prayerfully, humbly seeking those blessings as a victor versus a mere survivor. I recognize who I am apart from my husband's shame and acknowledge my new identity as a person uninhibited by my past adversities. My journey has revealed a metamorphosis of strength and resilience, layer by layer, and has unveiled a new compassion to others who have experienced addiction trauma. My hope is to share my story with encouragement to other survivors so that they too may discover their hidden beauty and purpose beneath the pain.

And so, with that realization, I could finally say goodbye at Kyle's funeral as I read these final words:

Funeral Letter

In 2005, I said goodbye to the man I committed the rest of my life to after twenty-four years together as a couple, then husband

and wife. While this was a pivotal event for our family, I continued to pray for him as I knew God would take care of us, but He needed me to trust as He paved a path for Kyle that would either lead to his healing or his demise. The choice was Kyle's. And so, I trusted.

In the days, months, and even years that followed, I longed to communicate with Kyle, but the risk of codependent arguments was too great. And so, instead, I wrote him letters, often wetting the pages with tears as I grieved the lost love and the loss of our family as we once knew it. It was traumatic, second only to the tragedy of losing our son.

The tenth anniversary of our son Ryan's death was the September following our divorce. On that day, I wrote Kyle this letter to add to our story's ending. I will now read Kyle this letter as we bury some of his ashes at our son's resting place.

Dear Kyle,

Today is reminiscent of the tenth anniversary of our lives without our eldest son, Ryan. It is appropriately cloudy and gloomy with intermittent rain, much like my mood. Whereas for the previous nine years, we could console each other, even if only telepathically, this year marks more than a decade of healing from the tragedy. It marks the beginning of many more futures of this anniversary apart, feelings and memories no longer shared, as we now go in two separate directions on life's journey without Ryan and now without each other. Today, we should be comforting each other as the only two persons alive who intricately understood the other's agony over the love lost when this little boy died. Instead, we are adversaries, absent from communication or even compassion for the other parent's pain. This, my dear husband, is the true tragedy and a dishonor to the joy this little boy brought when he entered our lives.

Unlike you, I see his short life here on earth as a gift extinguished far too early but not without meaning. Tucked away in a memory file, safe and sound and readily available for the asking, are the joyous moments and pleasures our son brought to our lives. I remember these often and can now smile as the pain is replaced with acceptance as the final stage of my grief.

Upon his loss, my experience, although painful, taught me the value of life as finite and fragile. That lesson I bestowed on the sacrifices I made for my family before and after our marriage dissolved. It also provided my reason for awakening every day and braving the piercing pain to serve you and our children as the caring, providing wife and mother each of you deserved.

Although our future with Ryan ended, my love for you and our family eventually brought me healing. It also brought me to a place of pure acceptance of God's will and provision despite the darkness and devastation of loss. The greatest tragedy is that you could not see past this pain to the opportunities for our future. By making different choices, you could have built memories with those of us who remained and continued to love you through life's hardships.

Today, as I read you my final goodbye letter and share your body with the ground that protects Ryan, I pray that you will now find peace, ending the battle of addiction that robbed us all of what could have and should have been. Know that you were the love of my life, and I said YES to the man in uniform behind the ring who represented a future I could not say no to. We are hopeful that you asked God's forgiveness before your death and received the mercy of healing and rest from a loving God who intimately knows the pain of a lost son.

Eulogy

My name is Dr. David Parler, and I'm proud to say that Kyle was one of my childhood best friends. I'd like to share with you today a bit about my best friend and the person many of us knew as someone very unique and special.

"Kyle Leslie Lackey," was his roll call the first day of class every year, as if to say, "Which do you go by? Kyle or Leslie?" I can assure you; he preferred Kyle. But just wait until recess. He would be called "Leslie" on the playground, at least for the first few days of school.

I have known Kyle since the first grade. He and I began school together in Ms. Friedlander's class. We literally grew up together throughout our childhood. I remember in the first grade reading the Dick and Jane series. As a former military brat, Kyle read with a slight accent from his time in Germany. He quickly replaced his accent with a Southern drawl when they returned home to the South.

We grew up together, studied together, planned our class schedules together, and we were partners on the debate team together through high school. We then graduated together, but then went our separate ways to college. I went to medical school, and he began a new career in the Air Force after his commencement, alongside his new bride.

Subjected to alcohol abuse, Kyle did not have an optimal home life. However, he never used this as an anchor. Instead, he pulled up his bootstraps, and he succeeded academically. I recall him proudly delivering a speech as a top 1 percent honor graduate, the number three graduate in his class, as he quoted the poetry of Alfred, Lord Tennyson, "To strive, to seek, to find, and not to yield."

I remember well that day he delivered that speech. Kyle truly set the example to others as he strived to attain greatness. He sought, he found, but how I wish so deeply he had not yielded. And that should be a warning to us all of temptations that we must guard ourselves against continually, and then seek help immediately when we are in trouble. Kyle would want the lessons of his misfortune to be used toward what's best for each of us, even if Kyle did not have the strength to achieve what was best for himself.

Kyle had a lot to be proud of. He took pride in his academic success and was the first in his family to achieve a college degree. He was offered full scholarships by the prestigious Citadel as well as the Navy and Air Force. He was proud of his accomplishments on the debate and tennis teams. He was the proud recipient of the Rotary Award given to the outstanding rising senior at our high school. He was proud of his military service and his first job. He was very proud of his wife, and I know proud of his children.

The Kyle I knew was a great young man. He had a heart of gold, and would give you the shirt off his back, literally. He was kind, caring, and empathetic. I'm sorry that I lost touch with Kyle after he moved to Texas. He wrestled with issues that I know haunted him and were not fair to his family. I know now that he had many battles that he fought like an illness, but they would not go away. But when I think back all those years ago as we grew up alongside each other, I cannot help but believe that I knew the real Kyle. I feel like I truly knew his heart and his soul. When his son Ryan died, he made it a point to tell me that Ryan had been baptized. He was very proud of that as well and recognized its significance and importance. His personal goal was to contribute his positive influence on all his relationships. The Kyle I knew is his legacy.

As I was thinking of what I was going to say while driving here this morning, I caught the lyrics of a song on the radio by a popular Christian songwriter. It enlightened me that each of us is broken in our own way. Our brokenness is customized to our life challenges. Some of us contend with these more than others. But we are all broken together; all of us, and in need of forgiveness from others, and in need of redemption by God.

Kyle Leslie Lackey: May you rest in peace. I love you like a brother.

Chapter 12

Anniversary Final Letter of Goodbye

Verse of Reflection

We are hard pressed on every side, but not crushed; perplexed, but not in despair; persecuted, but not abandoned; struck down, but not destroyed.

—2 Corinthians 4:8–9

From the desk of Kathryn Lackey . . .

One Last Goodbye

Dear Kyle,

I write this final letter on the first anniversary of your death last year, November 10th, 2020. Many might assume my vengeance is now fulfilled with you now dead. They cannot find reason nor fathom the depths of my loss and infinite grief of regret. Only when people have lived through the trauma of addiction's fury can they fully understand its destruction to even the most picture-perfect lives.

When your shroud fell, unraveling the secret life of a chronic sexual addiction, I divorced you to protect our family. However, my quest to survive never replaced my feelings for you. Refocused obligations faded the memories and soothed my scars. I stored them away in a memory box only to open during private, opportune moments when I had time to cry. But upon your passing, the lock on that memory box weakened and fell ajar. I have regular flashbacks of the man you once were and the beautiful life we shared. Some days, I get distracted by the reality of how I've lost you once again, now to death, after losing you and our wonderful life with our children.

I remember your charismatic nature and smile, the sound of your laugh, the trusting grip of your hand, your soft emerald eyes, and your smell when you drew close. You were my life's gift, my officer and a gentleman. I remember the treasures of you placing each of our three children on my chest after they left my body. Then, when we faced our deepest sorrow together, I will never forget how much I loved and respected you when we said goodbye at the funeral of our eldest son at age five. We were the only two people who understood each other's agony. I felt completely one with you as we attempted to reconstruct our family without Ryan. You were the myriad of strength, my soul mate and protector amid our loss. I was yours forever, and a large part of my heart will always belong to you.

As I open our memory box on the anniversary of your death, our times together have surfaced again as reminders of the damage caused by your secrets. My life is somewhat hollow as I transition into the next half of my life without you. We deserved to grow old alongside each other. Our children deserved the wonderful, loving, fun father they once knew. They were barely teens when you left for prison.

My heart aches when I recall you sitting at my bedside in college when I became ill during our freshman year. You remained loyal throughout my health struggles and academic recovery toward the rewards of graduation. You loved me throughout the trials of our courtship. We committed to a future together. Our slow wedding dance on a warm autumn day turned into frigid nights in our basement apartment. From there, we moved to beautiful homes built on love and filled with the sounds of family and laughter.

Then, like a thief in the night, you masked your addiction behind that man we all knew, giving it the power to annihilate everything. The man I loved, the father of my children, slowly faded away. The warm, wonderful, exuberant man I married was then replaced with someone evil, controlled by addiction's lies and self-destruction. On that day of revelation, your choices destroyed everything we built together, the lives we loved, and the future we were yet to live.

As our kids and I laid you to rest, accompanied by close friends and family, I looked down on the graves of the brother and your parents buried beside you, each life also lost tragically to the grip of addiction. Sadly, each life was extinguished prematurely. The power of addiction changed those people we loved, ended their lives, and scarred the lives of those close at heart.

This year, as I recall the phone call of that sad day informing me of your death, I repeat my goodbyes to the man who changed my life. I've experienced our marriage promise "for better and for worse" due to you. Where hate and anger could easily fill my soul, I have only sadness and regret for your choices and compassion for the man I once loved.

As I say goodbye this one last time through the writing of this book, I pray that God will not permit your life to be lost to shame but instead be purposeful in its lessons. My prayer is that our story will help others to find courage and strength through the suffering of a partner's addiction and embrace God throughout their journey to a newness of self.

With all my love,

Kathy

Bibliography

Berkowitz, Steve. "NCAA Revenue Returned to $1.15 Billion in 2021, but Prospect of Pandemic Impacts Looms." *USA Today* (February 3, 2022). https://www.usatoday.com/story/sports/2022/02/02/ncaa-revenue-up-but-pandemic-impacts-loom-basketball-tournament/9313735002/.

Carnes, Patrick J. *Out of the Shadows: Understanding Sexual Addiction.* Center City: Hazelden, 2001.

Grubbs, Joshua B., et al. "Porndemic? A Longitudinal Study of Pornography Use Before and During the COVID-19 Pandemic in a Nationally Representative Sample of Americans." *Archives of Sexual Behavior* 51, no.1 (2021): 123–37, https://doi.org/10.1007/s10508-021-02077-7.

Stevenson, Robert Louis. *Strange Case of Dr Jeckyll and Mr Hyde.* London: Longmans, Green, and Co., 1886.

"Top 100: The Most Visited Websites in the US [2022 Top Websites Edition]." *Semrush* (blog). Accessed March 8, 2023. https://www.semrush.com/blog/most-visited-websites/.

Kathryn's Story

For nearly twenty years, Kathryn Lackey has flourished designing interiors while enjoying her niche and passion for kitchen and bath design. In this haven, she plays in her sandbox, totally secure to create beauty for others as she disempowers the shame and obstacles once presented by her past.

Purely meant as a survival job following trauma and divorce from her husband's sexual addiction, she began her design career in a flooring sales role in 2006 during an economic recession. After eighteen months in her position, she chose unemployment for her unwillingness to work after nightly closings to instead care for her children as a sole parent. Soon following, she was introduced to the world of kitchen design as a cabinet specialist where she discovered design therapy during her life's greatest hardships. While growing her talent, she ran her parent's real estate investments as a second job while caring afar for her mother diagnosed with Alzheimer's. Following her mother's death in 2009, she inherited a third job as executor and spent the following three years renovating and liquidating multiple properties long-distance while simultaneously raising her two teenagers.

Kathryn's aspirations and efforts to return to her previous career in advertising became a distant hope as she juggled her many responsibilities, dedicated to the demands of her family following loss. She carried the burdens of shame battling self-doubt, belittlement, and discouragement as she attempted to find security and seal her past. Rising into district management, all with the rewards of a flat financial future, she finally woke up to her true potential in 2019, discovering entrepreneurship including all its rigors and ultimate fulfillments. But it first required a determination of faith in her true value apart from the past shames that halted her true potential.

Now at a place in life where her purpose and passion is to help others on a similar walk, her desires are to continue empowering women to find freedom from their past, personal success, and confidence through healing. She enjoys collaborating with other business-minded women who believe God has a plan for each individual, challenging them to excel beyond their adversities toward personal and financial accomplishment as His gifts of faith in the woman they were innately created to become.

Kathryn is the proud mother of two surviving children, Katie and Grayson, who gave purpose to her tenacity and strength to discover a new life beyond her pain. She focuses her time on implementing her vision for her future and design business as she reunites with her kids in Dallas following the death of her former husband. Her joys are quality time with family, exercise, movie nights, and all things design.

You can get more information to propel your personal journey by visiting her website at Kathrynmlackey.com. To learn more about her design business, visit HeartofHomeDesigns. com. You can also follow her on social media at:

Facebook:	facebook.com/kathryn.m.lackey/
Twitter:	@KMLackeyauthor
Instagram:	instagram.com/kathryn_m_lackey/
LinkedIn:	linkedin.com/feed/update/urn:li:share:720602 4374074687489/